CHINESE
in 10 minutes a day®

by Kristine Kershul, M.A., University of California, Santa Barbara

Consultant: Jiemin Wu

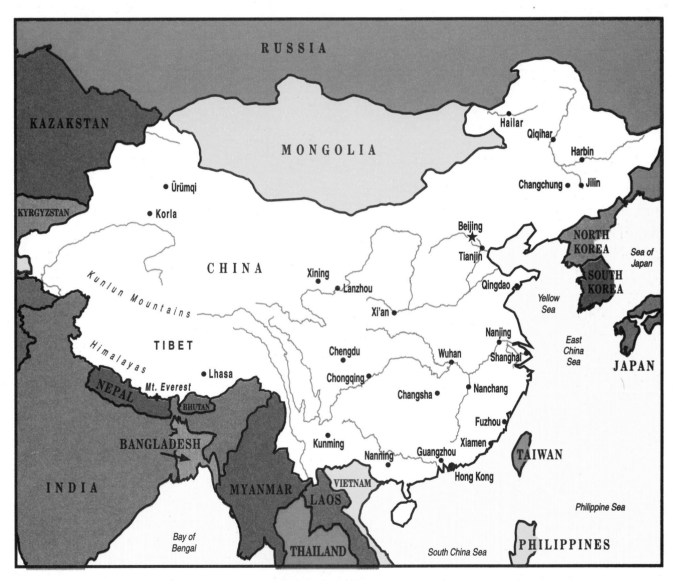

Bilingual Books, Inc.
1719 West Nickerson Street, Seattle, WA 98119
Tel: (206) 284-4211 Fax: (206) 284-3660
www.10minutesaday.com

Third printing, December 2004

Can you say this?

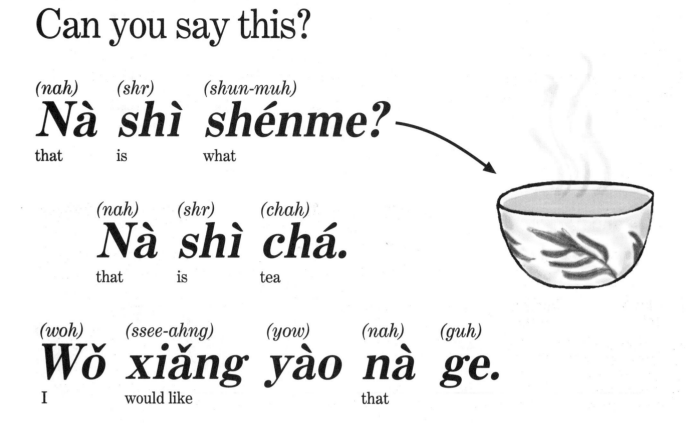

(nah) (shr) (shun-muh)
Nà shì shénme?
that   is   what

(nah) (shr) (chah)
Nà shì chá.
that   is   tea

(woh) (ssee-ahng) (yow) (nah) (guh)
Wǒ xiǎng yào nà ge.
I   would like   that

If you can say this, you can learn to speak Chinese. You will be able to easily order beer, lunch, tea, theater tickets, or anything else you wish. With your best Chinese accent, you simply ask **"Nà shì shénme?"** *(nah) (shr) (shun-muh)* and, upon learning what it is, you can order it with **"Wǒ xiǎng yào nà ge,"** *(woh) (ssee-ahng) (yow) (nah) (guh)*. Sounds easy, doesn't it?

The purpose of this book is to give you an **immediate** speaking ability in Chinese. More people speak some form of Chinese as their native language than any other language in the world. This book is based on **Pǔtōnghuà** *(poo-tohng-hwah)* meaning "common language." **Pǔtōnghuà** is modern, standardized Chinese and derives largely from Mandarin Chinese, the Beijing dialect of Chinese. To help you master these new sounds, this book offers a unique and easy system of pronunciation above each word which walks you through learning Chinese.

If you are planning a trip or moving to where Chinese is spoken, you will be leaps ahead of everyone if you take just a few minutes a day to learn the easy key words that this book offers. Start with Step 1 and don't skip around. Each day work as far as you can comfortably go in those 10 minutes. Don't overdo it. Some days you might want to just review. If you forget a word, you can always look it up in the glossary. Spend your first 10 minutes studying the map on the previous page. And yes, have fun learning your new language.

As you work through the Steps, always use the special features which only this series offers. This book contains sticky labels and flash cards, free words, puzzles and quizzes. When you have completed this book, cut out the menu guide and take it along on your trip.

1 Pīnyīn
(peen-yeen)

Pīnyīn is a system of spelling Chinese using the Roman alphabet. Throughout this book you will find an easy pronunciation guide above all new words. Practice these sounds with the examples given below which are mostly provinces or cities in China you might wish to visit. Refer to this Step whenever you need help, but remember, spend no longer than 10 minutes a day.

Chinese has four basic tones. The first time you work through this book, do not worry about them. Learn your vocabulary *first*. Once you learn the words, go back and practice with the tones.

Tone 1 is even. The voice produces a flat, somewhat higher pitch than normal. → **ā** **ă** ← Tone 3 is falling and rising. The voice drops from a normal pitch to a lower pitch and then rises again.

Tone 2 is rising. The voice rises from a normal to a higher pitch. → **á** **à** ← Tone 4 is falling. The voice falls from a high to a low pitch.

Pīnyīn letter	English sound	Examples	Write it here
a	ah	**Ānhuī** *(ahn-hway)*	
b	b	**Běijīng** *(bay-jeeng)*	
c	*(as in cats)* ts	**Cāngyánshān** *(tsahng-yahn-shahn)*	
ch	ch	**Chángshā** *(chahng-shah)*	*Chángshā, Chángshā*
d	d	**Hăinán Dăo** *(hi-nahn)(dow)* island	
e *(varies)*	uh	**Érhăi Hú** *(ur-hi)(hoo)* lake	
	(as in let) eh	**Éméishān** *(eh-may-shahn)*	
f	f	**Fújiàn** *(foo-jee-ahn)*	
g	g	**Gānsù** *(gahn-soo)*	
h	h	**Húnán** *(hoo-nahn)*	
i *(varies)*	ee	**Xī'ān** *(ssee-ahn)*	
	r	**Shíwān** *(shr-wahn)*	
	uh	**Zībó** *(zuh-bwoh)*	
	ih	**Sīmătái Chángchéng** *(sih-mah-tie)(chahng-chuhng)* Great Wall	
j	j	**Jílín** *(jee-leen)*	
k	k	**Kūnmíng** *(koon-meeng)*	
l	l	**Lāsà** *(lah-sah)*	
m	m	**Nèi Ménggŭ** *(nay)(muhng-goo)* Inner Mongolia	
n	n	**Nánjīng** *(nahn-jeeng)*	
o *(varies)*	oh	**Tóngjiāng** *(tohng-jee-ahng)*	

Pīnyīn letter	English sound	Examples	Write it here
o	woh	**Fóshān** (*fwoh-shahn*)	_____
p	p	**Pánshān** (*pahn-shahn*)	_____
q	ch	**Qīngdǎo** (*cheeng-dow*)	_____
r	r	**Hāěrbīn** (*hah-ur-been*)	_____
s	s	**Sìchuān** (*sih-chwahn*)	_____
sh	sh	**Shànghǎi** (*shahng-hi*)	_____
t	t	**Tiānjīn** (*tee-ahn-jeen*)	_____
u *(varies)*	oo	**Wúhú** (*woo-hoo*)	_____
	oo-we	**Yúlín** (*yoo-we-leen*)	_____
w	w	**Wǔhàn** (*woo-hahn*)	_____
x	*(a gentle hissing sound)* ss	**Xiāng Gǎng** (*ssee-ahng*)(*gahng*) Hong Kong	_____
y	y	**Yúnnán** (*yoon-nahn*)	_____
z	z	**Zōuxiàn** (*zoh-ssee-ahn*)	_____
zh	j	**Zhèjiāng** (*juh-jee-ahng*)	_____

Many of the following sounds were used in the above examples. Here is a chance to practice these new sounds and to learn your first ten Chinese words. Don't forget to have fun learning your new language.

ai	I / eye	*(hi)* **hǎi** sea	**ua** *(varies)*	wah	*(hwah)* **huà** language	
ao	*(as in how)* ow / ao	*(how)* **hǎo** good		oo-ah	*(yoo-ahn)* **yuán** unit of Chinese currency	
ei	ay	*(hay)* **hēi** black	**uai**	why	*(hwhy)* **huài** bad	
ou	oh	*(goh)* **gǒu** dog	**ui**	way	*(hway)* **huī** gray	
ü	oo-we	*(noo-we)* **nǚ** female	**uo**	woh	*(hwoh)* **huǒ** fire	

Regarding the phonetics, remember Chinese is spoken in a variety of ways. Think about how different British and American English sound. In Chinese the tones will vary or can even be absent. Sometimes words will be combined instead of being written separately. Don't let these things surprise you.

* **r** is similar to a little growl, so **shí** (*shr*) sounds almost like the English "sure"
* **oh/woh** sometimes it can be difficult to tell the difference between these sounds

The easiest and best possible phonetics have been chosen for each individual word. Pronounce the phonetics just as you see them. Don't over-analyze them.

2   Key Question Words

When you arrive in **Běijīng** *(bay-jeeng)* or **Shànghǎi** *(shahng-hi)* the very first thing you will need to do is **ask**

questions — "Where **(nǎr)** *(nahr)* is the bus stop?" "**Nǎr** *(nahr)* can I exchange money?" "**Nǎr** *(nahr)* is the
    where   where

lavatory?" "**Nǎr** is a restaurant?" "**Nǎr** do I catch a taxi?" "**Nǎr** is a good hotel?" "**Nǎr** is my

luggage?" — and the list will go on and on for the entire length of your visit. In Chinese, there

are NINE KEY QUESTION WORDS to learn. For example, the nine key question words will

help you find out exactly what you are ordering in a restaurant before you order it — and not

after the surprise (or shock!) arrives. Take a few minutes to study and practice saying the nine

key question words listed below. Then cover the Chinese with your hand and fill in each of the

blanks with the matching Chinese **cí.** *(tsih)*
                                       word

(nahr)
NǍR   =   WHERE _____

(shun-muh)
SHÉNME   =   WHAT _____

(shay)
SHÉI   =   WHO *shéi, shéi, shéi, shéi*

(way-shun-muh)
WÈISHÉNME   =   WHY _____

(shun-muh)   *(shr-hoh)*
SHÉNME SHÍHOU   =   WHEN _____

(zuhn-muh)
ZĚNME   =   HOW _____

(dwoh-shao)
DUŌSHAO   =   HOW MUCH _____
                               HOW MANY

(jee)
JǏ   =   HOW MANY _____

(nay)
NĚI   =   WHICH _____

5

Now test yourself to see if you really can keep these **cí** *(tsih)* words straight in your mind. Draw lines between the **Zhōngwén** *(jwong-wuhn)* Chinese language **cí** *(tsih)* words and their English equivalents below.

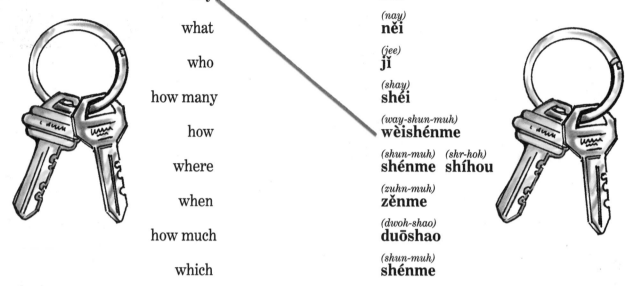

why	**nǎr** *(nahr)*
what	**něi** *(nay)*
who	**jǐ** *(jee)*
how many	**shéi** *(shay)*
how	**wèishénme** *(way-shun-muh)*
where	**shénme shíhou** *(shun-muh) (shr-hoh)*
when	**zěnme** *(zuhn-muh)*
how much	**duōshao** *(dwoh-shao)*
which	**shénme** *(shun-muh)*

Examine the following questions containing these **cí** *(tsih)*. Practice the sentences out loud and then practice by copying the Chinese in the blanks underneath each question.

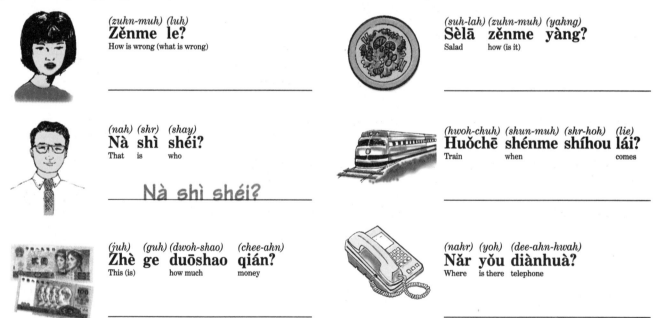

Zěnme le? *(zuhn-muh) (luh)*
How is wrong (what is wrong)

_____

Sèlā zěnme yàng? *(suh-lah) (zuhn-muh) (yahng)*
Salad   how (is it)

_____

Nà shì shéi? *(nah) (shr) (shay)*
That is   who

Nà shì shéi?

Huǒchē shénme shíhou lái? *(hwoh-chuh) (shun-muh) (shr-hoh) (lie)*
Train   when   comes

_____

Zhè ge duōshao qián? *(juh) (guh) (dwoh-shao) (chee-ahn)*
This (is) how much   money

_____

Nǎr yǒu diànhuà? *(nahr) (yoh) (dee-ahn-hwah)*
Where is there telephone

_____

"Nǎr" *(nahr)* will be your most used question **cí** *(tsih)*. Say each of the following Chinese sentences aloud. Then write out each sentence without looking at the example. If you don't succeed on the first try, don't give up. Just practice each sentence until you are able to do it easily. Remember **"ai"** is pronounced like the word "eye" or "I" and **"ao"** is pronounced "ow" as in "how."

(nahr) (yoh) (tsuh-swoh)
Nǎr yǒu cèsuǒ?
where is there lavatory

(nahr) (yoh) (choo-zoo-chuh)
Nǎr yǒu chūzūchē?
where is there taxi

(yoh) (gohng-gohng-chee-chuh)
Nǎr yǒu gōnggòngqìchē?
bus

_____   Nǎr yǒu chūzūchē?   _____

(fahn-gwahn)
Nǎr yǒu fànguǎn?
restaurant

(yeen-hahng)
Nǎr yǒu yínháng?
bank

(loo-we-gwahn)
Nǎr yǒu lǚguǎn?
hotel

Chinese and English are obviously very different languages, but some things are actually easier in Chinese. Notice how similar questions and statements are in Chinese.

(nahr) (yoh) (tsuh-swoh)
Nǎr yǒu cèsuǒ? (question)
where is there lavatory

(juhr) (yoh) (tsuh-swoh)
Zhèr yǒu cèsuǒ. (statement)
here

(shun-muh)
Shénme is a useful question **cí**. From **shénme,** come other question word combinations.
what

shénme shíhou *(shr-hoh)* = what time/when _____ shénme shíhou, shénme shíhou _____

shénme dìfāng *(dee-fahng)* = what place/where _____

shénme rén *(ruhn)* = what person/who _____

Notice how these groups of words are built around a common element. Here it is "zi" pronounced "zuh."

☑ **chāzi** *(chah-zuh)* .... fork   _chāzi, chāzi, chāzi, chāzi, chāzi_

☐ **bēizi** *(bay-zuh)* .... cup, mug _____

☐ **dāozi** *(dow-zuh)* .... knife   _____

☐ **kuàizi** *(kwhy-zuh)* .... chopsticks *zi* _____

Additional fun **cí** like these will appear at the bottom of the following pages in a yellow color band. Say each **cí** aloud and then write out the **Zhōngwén cí** *(jwong-wuhn)* in the blank to the right.
Chinese language

(jwong-gwoh) *(hwah)* *(tsih)* *(jwong-gwoh)* *(hwah)* *(juh)* *(nah)*
Zhōngguó huà does not have **cí** for "the" and "a." Instead, **Zhōngguó huà** uses **zhè** and **nà**
China   language   this   that

(jwong-gwoh) *(juh)* *(nah)*
for "the" and nothing for "a." In **Zhōngguó huà, zhè** and **nà** reflect the item's distance from
                                                 this   that

the speaker.

(juh) *(shoo)*   *(nah)* *(shoo)*   *(juh)* *(jee)*   *(nah)* *(jee)*
zhè shū vs. **nà shū**   **zhè jī** vs. **nà jī**
this   book   that   book   this   chicken   that   chicken

(juh) *(yoo-we)*   *(nah)* *(yoo-we)*   *(juh)* *(dee-ahn-hwah)*   *(nah)* *(dee-ahn-hwah)*
zhè yú vs. **nà yú**   **zhè diànhuà** vs. **nà diànhuà**
this   fish   that   this   telephone   that

(juh) *(nah)*
In addition to **zhè** and **nà,** Chinese has "measure words" (M) or "counting words" for everything.
          this   that

(buhn) *(tsih)* *(buhn)*
Běn is an example of a Chinese measure **cí. Běn,** meaning "bound together," is used with words
(M)   (M)

like "book" and "magazine."

(yee) *(buhn)* *(shoo)*   *(yee)* *(buhn)* *(zah-jihr)*
yì běn shū   **yì běn zázhì**
one   (bound)   book   one   (M)   magazine

Often Chinese "measure words" cannot be translated into English. Don't worry about them. You

can easily identify these "measure words" by the (M) underneath them.

In Step 2 you were introduced to the Nine Key QuestionWords. These nine words are the basics, the most essential building blocks for learning Chinese. Throughout this book you will come across keys asking you to fill in the missing question word. Use this opportunity not only to fill in the blank on that key, but to review all your question words. Play with the new sounds, speak slowly and have fun.

☐ **chē** *(chuh)*	. . . .	vehicle	
☐ **chēpái** *(chuh-pie)*	. . . .	license plate	
☐ **chēzhàn** *(chuh-jahn)*	. . . .	vehicle/bus stop	
☐ **jípǔchē** *(jee-poo-chuh)*	. . . .	jeep	
☐ **miànbāochē** *(mee-ahn-bao-chuh)*	. . . .	van	

车
chē

Before you proceed with this Step, situate yourself comfortably in your living room. Now look

around you. Can you name the things that you see in this **kètīng** *(kuh-teeng)* in Chinese? You can probably
living room

guess **shāfā** *(shah-fah)* means "sofa." Let's learn the rest of them. After practicing these **cí** *(tsih)* out loud,

write them in the blanks below.

(chwahng-hoo)
chuānghù
window

(dung)
dēng _____
lamp

(shah-fah)
shāfā _____
sofa

(yee-zuh)
yǐzi _____
chair

(dee-bahn)
dìbǎn _____
floor

(jwoh-zuh)
zhuōzi ___ zhuōzi, zhuōzi, zhuōzi _____
table

(muhn)
mén _____
door

(jwong)
zhōng _____
clock

(chah-jee)
chájī _____
coffee table

(dee-ahn-hwah)
diànhuà _____
telephone

(hwahr)
huàr
picture

Remember that **Zhōngguó huà** *(hwah)* has no word for "the." Use **zhè** *(juh)* or **nà** *(nah)* before the object to
China

indicate something in particular or use a number. Even easier, don't use anything at all! Now

open your **shū** *(shoo)* to the sticky labels on page 17 and later on page 35. Peel off the first 11 labels
book

and proceed around the **kètīng** *(kuh-teeng)*, labeling these items in your **jiā** *(jee-ah)*. This will help to increase your
living room   home

Zhōngwén *(jwong-wuhn)* **cí** *(tsih)* power easily. Don't forget to say each **cí** as you attach the label.
Chinese language   word

Now ask yourself, "**Shāfā** *(shah-fah)* **zài** *(zi)* **nǎr?**" *(nahr)* and point at it while you answer, "**Shāfā zài** *(zi)* **zhèr.**" *(juhr)*
sofa   is   where   is   here

Continue on down the list above until you feel comfortable with these **xīn cí.** *(sseen)*
new

❏	**diànchē** *(dee-ahn-chuh)*	trolley	
❏	**huǒchē** *(hwoh-chuh)*	train	车
❏	**qìchē** *(chee-chuh)*	car	
❏	**sānlúnchē** *(sahn-loon-chuh)*	pedicab	*chē*
❏	**zìxíngchē** *(zih-sseeng-chuh)*	bicycle	

(fahng-zuh)
fángzi = house

Fángzi *(zi)* **zài** *(juhr)* **zhèr.**
　　　　　is　　here

(shoo-fahng)
shūfáng
study/den

(yoo-we-shr)
yùshì
bathroom

(choo-fahng)
chúfáng
kitchen

(shway-fahng)
shuìfáng
bedroom

(fahn-teeng)
fàntīng
dining room

(kuh-teeng)
kètīng
living room

(chuh-koo)
chēkù
garage

(dee-ssee-ah-shr)
dìxiàshì
basement

While learning these **xīn** *(sseen)* **cí,** *(tsih)* let's not forget:
　　　　　　　　　　 new　　 words

(chee-chuh)
qìchē
car

(sahn-loon-chuh)
sānlúnchē
pedicab

(zih-sseeng-chuh)
zìxíngchē
bicycle

_____　　_____　　_____

☐	**bǐ** *(bee)*	pen, writing instrument	_____
☐	**bǐjì** *(bee-jee)*	to take notes	_____
☐	**bǐjī** *(bee-jee)*	handwriting	_____
☐	**bǐjìběn** *(bee-jee-buhn)*	notebook	_____
☐	**bǐxīn** *(bee-sseen)*	pen/pencil refill	_____

笔
bǐ

(mao)
māo
cat

(hwah-yoo-ahn)
huāyuán
garden

(hwahr)
huār (**huàr** means picture!)
flowers

huāyuán, huāyuán

(goh)
gǒu
dog

(yoh-twong)
yóutǒng
mailbox

(sseen)
xìn
letters

Peel off the next set of labels and wander through your **fángzi** *(fahng-zuh)* learning these **xīn cí** *(sseen) (tsih)*. It will
house   new

be somewhat difficult to label your **gǒu,** *(goh)* **huār** *(hwahr)* or **māo** *(mao)* but be creative. Practice by asking
dog   flowers   cat

yourself, "**Nǎr yǒu huāyuán?**" *(nahr) (yoh) (hwah-yoo-ahn)* and reply, "**Huāyuán zài zhèr.**" *(zi) (juhr)*
where is there   here

(yoh) (fahng-zuh)
Nǎr yǒu fángzi?
house

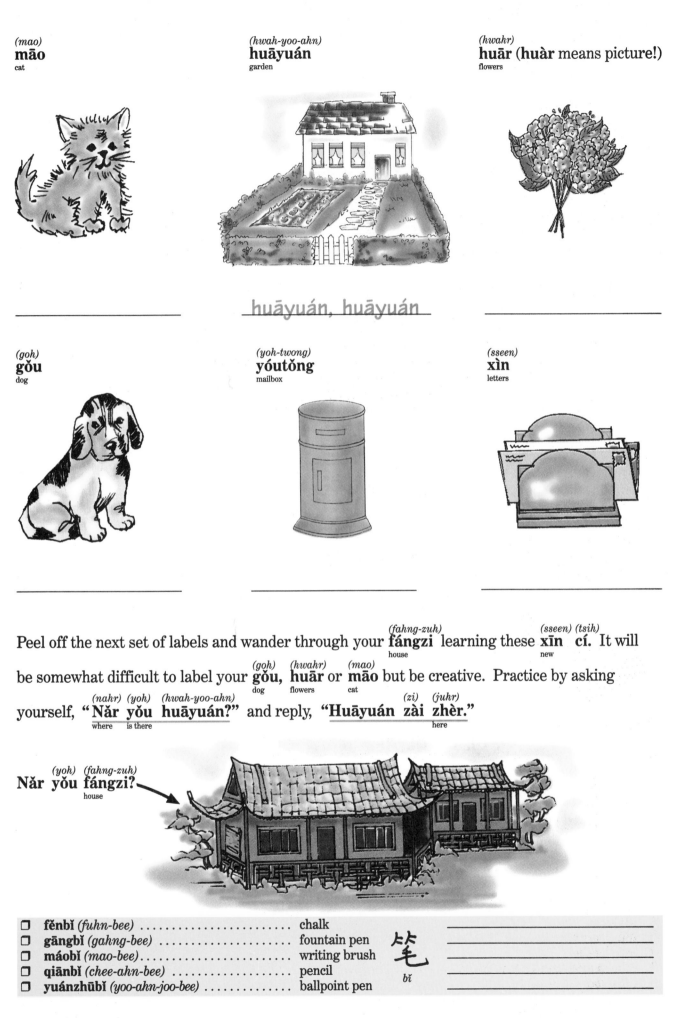

❏ **fěnbǐ** *(fuhn-bee)*	chalk	
❏ **gāngbǐ** *(gahng-bee)*	fountain pen	笔
❏ **máobǐ** *(mao-bee)*	writing brush	*bǐ*
❏ **qiānbǐ** *(chee-ahn-bee)*	pencil	
❏ **yuánzhūbǐ** *(yoo-ahn-joo-bee)*	ballpoint pen	

(yee) *(ur)* *(sahn)*
Yī, Èr, Sān!
one two three

Consider for a minute how important numbers are. How could you tell someone your phone number, your address or your hotel room if you had no numbers? And think of how difficult it would be if you could not understand the time, the price of a sandwich or the correct bus to take. When practicing the **shùzì** *(shoo-zih)* below, notice the similarities which have been underlined for you between **èr** *(ur)* and **shíèr,** *(shr-ur)* **qì** *(chee)* and **shíqī,** *(shr-chee)* and so on.
(two / twelve / seven / seventeen)
(numbers)

0	*(leeng)* **líng**	_____	10	*(shr)* **shí**	_____
1	*(yee)* **yī**	_____	11	*(shr-yee)* **shíyī**	_____
2	*(ur)* **èr**	_____	12	*(shr-ur)* **shíèr**	_____
3	*(sahn)* **sān**	_____	13	*(shr-sahn)* **shísān**	_____
4	*(sih)* **sì**	_____	14	*(shr-sih)* **shísì**	_____
5	*(woo)* **wǔ**	_____	15	*(shr-woo)* **shíwǔ**	_____
6	*(lee-oo)* **liù**	_____	16	*(shr-lee-oo)* **shíliù**	_____
7	*(chee)* **qī**	*qī, qī, qī, qī, qī*	17	*(shr-chee)* **shíqī**	_____
8	*(bah)* **bā**	_____	18	*(shr-bah)* **shíbā**	_____
9	*(jee-oo)* **jiǔ**	_____	19	*(shr-jee-oo)* **shíjiǔ**	_____
10	*(shr)* **shí**	_____	20	*(ur-shr)* **èrshí**	_____

☑	**diàn** *(dee-ahn)*	electricity	*diàn, diàn, diàn, diàn, diàn, diàn*
☐	**diànbào** *(dee-ahn-bao)*	telegram	_____
☐	**diànhuà** *(dee-ahn-hwah)*	telephone	_____
☐	**diànnǎo** *(dee-ahn-now)*	computer	_____
☐	**diàntǒng** *(dee-ahn-twong)*	flashlight	_____

diàn

Use these **shùzì** *(shoo-zih)* / numbers on a daily basis. Count to yourself in **Zhōngguó** *(jwong-gwoh)* **huà** *(hwah)* / language when you brush your teeth, exercise or commute to work. Fill in the blanks below according to the **shùzì** *(shoo-zih)* / numbers given in parentheses. Now is also a good time to learn these two very important phrases. *Note:* When you count, you use "**èr**" *(ur)* / two, but when you are asked "how many" or you say "two pencils" or "two books" you use "**liǎng**." *(lee-ahng)* / two

wǒ *(woh)* I **xiǎng** *(ssee-ahng)* **yào** *(yow)* would like _____

wǒmen *(woh-muhn)* we **xiǎng** *(ssee-ahng)* **yào** *(yow)* would like _____

Wǒ *(woh)* I **xiǎng** *(ssee-ahng)* **yào** *(yow)* would like _____ (10) **zhāng** *(jahng)* (M) **míngxìnpiàn.** *(meeng-sseen-pee-ahn)* postcards   **Duōshao?** *(dwoh-shao)* how much/how many _____ (10)

Wǒ xiǎng yào _____ (11) **zhāng yóupiào.** *(yoh-pee-ow)* (M) stamps   **Duōshao?** *(dwoh-shao)* _____ (11)

Wǒ xiǎng yào __bā__ (8) **zhāng** *(jahng)* **yóupiào.** *(yoh-pee-ow)* I   **Duōshao?** _____ (8)

Wǒ xiǎng yào _____ (2) **zhāng yóupiào.**   **Duōshao?** _____ (2)

Wǒmen *(woh-muhn)* we **xiǎng yào** _____ (9) **zhāng míngxìnpiàn.** *(meeng-sseen-pee-ahn)* (M) postcards   **Duōshao?** _____ (9)

Wǒmen xiǎng yào _____ (10) **zhāng míngxìnpiàn.**   **Duōshao?** _____ (10)

Wǒmen xiǎng yào _____ (3) **zhāng** *(jahng)* (M) **xìpiào.** *(ssee-pee-ow)* theater tickets   **Duōshao?** _____ (3)

Wǒ *(woh)* I **xiǎng yào** _____ (4) **zhāng xìpiào.**   **Duōshao?** _____ (4)

Wǒ xiǎng yào _____ (11) **zhāng xìpiào.**   **Duōshao?** _____ (11)

Wǒmen xiǎng yào _____ (6) **bēi** *(bay)* cup (M) **chá.** *(chah)* tea   **Duōshao?** _____ (6)

Wǒmen xiǎng yào _____ (5) **bēi** *(bay)* (M) **shuǐ.** *(shway)* water   (how many) _____ (5)

☐ **diànchí** *(dee-ahn-chee)* .... battery   _____

☐ **diànshì** *(dee-ahn-shr)* .... television   _____

☐ **diàntái** *(dee-ahn-tie)* .... radio station   电 _____

☐ **diàntī** *(dee-ahn-tee)* .... elevator, escalator   *diàn* _____

☐ **diànyǐng** *(dee-ahn-yeeng)* .... movie   _____

Now see if you can translate the following thoughts into **Zhōngwén**. *(jwong-wuhn)* The answers are provided upside down at the bottom of **zhèi yè**. *(juh-ay) (yeh)*
this page

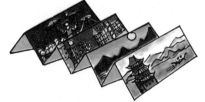

1. I would like seven postcards.

_____

2. I would like nine stamps.

_____

3. We would like four cups of tea.

_____

4. We would like three theater tickets.

_____

Review the **shùzì** *(shoo-zih)* 1 to 20. Write out your telephone number, fax number and cellular number.

Then write out a friend's telephone number and a relative's telephone number.

(2   0   6)   3   4   0   —   4   4   2   2

èr líng liù

(   )   —   _   _   _   _

_____

(   )   —   _   _   _   _

_____

6   (yahn-suh) Yánsè
colors

(yahn-suh)
Yánsè are the same in **Zhōngguó** as they are in **Měiguó** (may-gwoh) — they just have different **míngzì**. (meeng-zuh) In
colors   America   names

Zhōngguó, there are many different customs regarding **yánsè**. (yahn-suh) Let's learn the basic **yánsè** (yahn-suh) so
colors

when you are invited to someone's **fángzi** (fahng-zuh) and you want to bring flowers, you will be able to order
house

the color you want. Once you've learned the **yánsè,** (yahn-suh) quiz yourself. What color are your shoes?

Your eyes? Your hair? Your house?

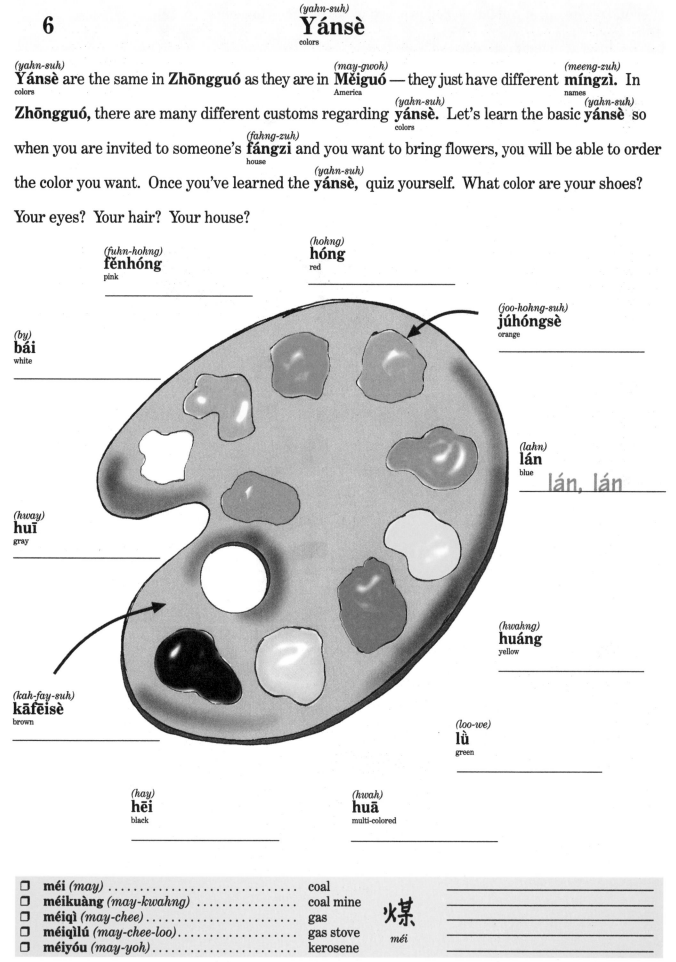

fěnhóng *(fuhn-hohng)*
pink
_____

hóng *(hohng)*
red
_____

júhóngsè *(joo-hohng-suh)*
orange
_____

bái *(by)*
white
_____

lán *(lahn)*
blue
lán, lán _____

huī *(hway)*
gray
_____

huáng *(hwahng)*
yellow
_____

kāfēisè *(kah-fay-suh)*
brown
_____

lǜ *(loo-we)*
green
_____

hēi *(hay)*
black
_____

huā *(hwah)*
multi-colored
_____

❏	**méi** *(may)*	....	coal	
❏	**méikuàng** *(may-kwahng)*	....	coal mine	煤 _____
❏	**méiqì** *(may-chee)*	....	gas	*méi*
❏	**méiqìlú** *(may-chee-loo)*	....	gas stove	
❏	**méiyóu** *(may-yoh)*	....	kerosene	

Peel off the next group of labels and proceed to label these **yánsè** in your **fángzi.** *(fahng-zuh)* Identify the

house

two or three dominant colors in the flags below.

Japan		Thailand	
South Korea		Canada	
People's Republic of China		United States	
New Zealand		Vietnam	
Australia		Singapore	
United Kingdom		Russia	
Laos		Indonesia	

Were you able to guess that **"kāfēi"** *(kah-fay)* is the **Zhōngwén cí** *(tsih)* for the beverage "coffee" and that the

word

cí "kāfēisè" *(kah-fay-suh)* actually means "coffee-colored?"

brown

_____ _____ **yǒu chūzūchē?**
(where) (where) *(yoh) (choo-zoo-chuh)*
taxi

_____ **Nà shì** _____ ?
(what) that *(shr)* (what)

☐ **xǐ** *(ssee)*	to wash	_____
☐ **xǐjiāojuǎn** *(ssee-jee-ow-joo-ahn)*	to develop (the) film	_____
☐ **xǐyī diàn** *(ssee-yee)(dee-ahn)*	laundry	_____
☐ **xǐyīfú** *(ssee-yee-foo)*	to do laundry	洗 _____
☐ **xǐzǎo** *(ssee-zow)*	to take a bath	xǐ

(dung) **dēng**	*(chee-chuh)* **qìchē**	*(fuhn-hohng)* **fěnhóng**	*(pee-jee-oo)* **píjiǔ**
(shah-fah) **shāfā**	*(sahn-loon-chuh)* **sānlúnchē**	*(hohng)* **hóng**	*(nee-oo-ni)* **niúnǎi**
(yee-zuh) **yǐzi**	*(zih-sseeng-chuh)* **zìxíngchē**	*(by)* **bái**	*(nee-oo-yoh)* **niúyóu**
(dee-bahn) **dìbǎn**	*(mao)* **māo**	*(joo-hohng-suh)* **júhóngsè**	*(yahn)* **yán**
(jwoh-zuh) **zhuōzi**	*(hwah-yoo-ahn)* **huāyuán**	*(lahn)* **lán**	*(hoo-jee-ow)* **hújiāo**
(muhn) **mén**	*(hwahr)* **huār**	*(hway)* **huī**	*(jee-oo-bay)* **jiǔbēi**
(jwong) **zhōng**	*(goh)* **gǒu**	*(hwahng)* **huáng**	*(bwoh-lee-bay)* **bōlíbēi**
(chah-jee) **chájī**	*(yoh-twong)* **yóutǒng**	*(kah-fay-suh)* **kāfēisè**	*(kwhy-zuh)* **kuàizi**
(dee-ahn-hwah) **diànhuà**	*(sseen)* **xìn**	*(hay)* **hēi**	*(bao-jihr)* **bàozhǐ**
(chwahng-hoo) **chuānghu**	**0** *(leeng)* **líng**	*(hwah)* **huā**	*(chah-bay)* **chábēi**
(hwahr) **huàr**	**1** *(yee)* **yī**	*(loo-we)* **lù**	*(tsahn-jeen)* **cānjīn**
(fahng-zuh) **fángzi**	**2** *(ur)* **èr**	*(neen)* **nín** *(jow)* **zhǎo**	*(chah-zuh)* **chāzi**
(shoo-fahng) **shūfáng**	**3** *(sahn)* **sān**	*(wahn-shahng)* **wǎnshàng** *(jee-ahn)* **jiàn**	*(pahn-zuh)* **pánzi**
(yoo-we-shr) **yùshì**	**4** *(sih)* **sì**	*(meeng-tee-ahn)* **míngtiān** *(jee-ahn)* **jiàn**	*(dow-zuh)* **dāozi**
(choo-fahng) **chúfáng**	**5** *(woo)* **wǔ**	*(wahn)* **wǎn** *(ahn)* **ān**	*(tahng-chr)* **tāngchí**
(shway-fahng) **shuǐfáng**	**6** *(lee-oo)* **liù**	*(zi-jee-ahn)* **zàijiàn**	*(gway-zuh)* **guìzi**
(fahn-teeng) **fàntīng**	**7** *(chee)* **qī**	*(nee)* **Nǐ** *(how)* **hǎo** *(mah)* **ma?**	*(chah)* **chá**
(kuh-teeng) **kètīng**	**8** *(bah)* **bā**	*(beeng-ssee-ahng)* **bīngxiāng**	*(kah-fay)* **kāfēi**
(chuh-koo) **chēkù**	**9** *(jee-oo)* **jiǔ**	*(loo-zuh)* **lúzi**	*(mee-ahn-bao)* **miànbāo**
(dee-ssee-ah-shr) **dìxiàshì**	**10** *(shr)* **shí**	*(jee-oo)* **jiǔ**	*(cheeng)* **qǐng**

STICKY LABELS

This book has over 150 special sticky labels for you to use as you learn new words. When you are introduced to one of these words, remove the corresponding label from these pages. Be sure to use each of these unique self-adhesive labels by adhering them to a picture, window, lamp, or whatever object they refer to. And yes, they are removable! The sticky labels make learning to speak Chinese much more fun and a lot easier than you ever expected. For example, when you look in the mirror and see the label, say

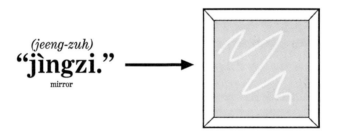

(jeeng-zuh)
"jìngzi."
mirror

Don't just say it once, say it again and again. And once you label the refrigerator, you should never again open that door without saying

(beeng-ssee-ahng)
"bīngxiāng."
refrigerator

By using the sticky labels, you not only learn new words, but friends and family learn along with you! The sooner you start, the sooner you can use these labels at home or work.

7 Qián
(chee-ahn)

money

Before starting this Step, go back and review Step 5. It is important that you can count to **èrshí** *(ur-shr)* twenty

without looking at the **shū** *(shoo)*. Let's learn the larger **shùzì** *(shoo-zih)* now. After practicing aloud the
book   numbers

Zhōngwén *(jwong-wuhn)* **shùzì** *(shoo-zih)* 10 through 1,000 below, write these **shùzì** *(shoo-zih)* in the blanks provided. Again, notice
Chinese

the similarities (underlined) between numbers such as **wǔ** *(woo)* (5), **shíwǔ** *(shr-woo)* (15), and **wǔshí** *(woo-shr)* (50). Don't

be surprised when you hear **liǎng** *(lee-ahng)* used for the number two, for example, **liǎngbǎi** *(lee-ahng-by)* or **èrbǎi** *(ur-by)*.
                                                                              two hundred   two hundred

First learn the numbers below, then you can practice all the numbers in between them!

10	**shí** *(shr)* _____		100	**yìbǎi** *(yee-by)* _____
20	**èrshí** *(ur-shr)* _____		200	**èrbǎi** _____
30	**sānshí** *(sahn-shr)* _____		300	**sānbǎi** _sānbǎi, sānbǎi_
40	**sìshí** *(sih-shr)* _____		400	**sìbǎi** _____
50	**wǔshí** *(woo-shr)* _____		500	**wǔbǎi** *(woo-by)* _____
60	**liùshí** *(lee-oo-shr)* _____		600	**liùbǎi** _____
70	**qīshí** *(chee-shr)* _____		700	**qībǎi** _____
80	**bāshí** *(bah-shr)* _____		800	**bābǎi** _____
90	**jiǔshí** *(jee-oo-shr)* _____		900	**jiǔbǎi** *(jee-oo-by)* _____
100	**yìbǎi** *(yee-by)* _____		1000	**yìqiān** *(yee-chee-ahn)* _____

Here are **liǎng** *(lee-ahng)* important phrases to go with all these **shùzì** *(shoo-zih)*. Say them out loud over and over
two

and then write them out twice as many times.

wǒ yǒu *(woh)(yoh)* _____
I   have

wǒmen yǒu *(woh-muhn)* _____
we   have

Note: In **Zhōngguó huà**, "**yǒu** *(yoh)*" means both "to have" and "there is/there are." It may seem a

bit odd at first, but you'll get the hang of it. Don't worry.

❑ **nián** *(nee-ahn)*	year	年 _____
❑ **jīn nián** *(jeen)(nee-ahn)*	this year	_____
❑ **míng nián** *(meeng)(nee-ahn)*.	next year	_____
❑ **qù nián** *(chee-oo)(nee-ahn)*	last year	_____
❑ **sān nián** *(sahn)(nee-ahn)*	three years	*nián*

The unit of currency in **Zhōngguó** *(jwong-gwoh)* China is the **yuán** *(yoo-ahn)*. Just as in **Měiguó** *(may-gwoh)* America where a dollar can be broken down into 100 pennies, the **yuán** *(yoo-ahn)* can be broken down into 100 **fēn** *(fuhn)*. The **yuán** *(yoo-ahn)* can also be broken down into 10 **jiǎo** *(jee-ow)* or **máo** *(mao)*. **Jiǎo** *(jee-ow)*, **máo** *(mao)* and **fēn** *(fuhn)* are also called **língqián** *(leeng-chee-ahn)* change. Currency regulations do change frequently. Check with your local foreign-exchange office about exchanging your currency for **yuán** *(yoo-ahn)*. Study the pictures below to familiarize yourself with the various bills and coins. **Fēn** do exist, but are used infrequently. Confused? Think of a **jiǎo** *(jee-ow)* as a dime, as there are ten **jiǎo** *(jee-ow)* to a **yuán** just as there are ten dimes to an American dollar.

Qián *(chee-ahn)*
bills

Língqián *(leeng-chee-ahn)*
change

yì yuán / kuài *(yee) (yoo-ahn) (kwhy)*
one

yì jiǎo / máo *(yee) (jee-ow) (mao)*
one

liǎng yuán / kuài *(lee-ahng) (yoo-ahn) (kwhy)*
two

èr jiǎo / máo *(ur) (jee-ow) (mao)*
two

wǔ yuán / kuài *(woo) (kwhy)*
five

wǔ jiǎo / máo *(woo)*
five

shí yuán / kuài *(shr)*
ten

yì fēn *(yee) (fuhn)*
one

wǔshí yuán / kuài *(woo-shr)*
fifty

èr fēn *(ur) (fuhn)*
two

yìbǎi yuán / kuài *(yee-by)*
one hundred

wǔ fēn *(woo)*
five

❑ **là** *(lah)*	wax		
❑ **làbǐ** *(lah-bee)*	crayon	蜡	
❑ **làtái** *(lah-tie)*	candlestick		
❑ **làzhǐ** *(lah-jihr)*	wax paper	*là*	
❑ **làzhú** *(lah-joo)*	candle		

Review the *(shoo-zih)(shr)* **shùzì shí** through *(yee-chee-ahn)* **yìqiān** again. Now, in *(jwong-wuhn)* **Zhōngwén**, how do you say "twenty-two" or "fifty-three"? You actually do a bit of arithmetic – 5 times 10 plus 3 equals 53. (*wǔ* x *shí* + *sān* = *wǔshísān*) See if you can say and write out the *(shoo-zih)* **shùzì** on *(juh-ay)* **zhèi** *(yeh)* **yè**. The answers *(zi)* **zài** the bottom of the *(yeh)* **yè**.

numbers ten — one thousand — Chinese — this — are (at) — page

1. _____
(25 = 2 x 10 + 5)

2. _____
(83 = 8 x 10 + 3)

3. _____
(47 = 4 x 10 + 7)

4. _____
(96 = 9 x 10 + 6)

Now, how would you say the following in *(jwong-gwoh)* **Zhōngguó** *(hwah)* **huà?**

Chinese — language

5. _____
(I have 80 yuán.)

6. _____
(We have 72 yuán.)

To ask how much something costs in **Zhōngguó huà,** one asks — *(dwoh-shao)* **Duōshao** *(chee-ahn)* **qián?**

how much — money

(ssee-ahn-zi) **Xiànzài** you try it. _____
now — (How much money/How much does that cost?)

Answer the following questions based on the numbers in parentheses.

7. *(nah)(guh)(dwoh-shao)(chee-ahn)* **Nà ge duōshao qián?** *(nah)(guh)* **Nà ge** _____ *(yoo-ahn)* **yuán.**
that — how much — money — that — (10)

8. *(buhn)(shoo)* **Nà běn shū duōshao qián? Nà běn shū** _____ **yuán.**
(M) book — (M) — (17)

9. *(jahng)(meeng-sseen-pee-ahn)* **Nà zhāng míngxìnpiàn duōshao qián? Nà zhāng míngxìnpiàn** _____ **yuán.**
(M) postcard — (M) — (20)

10. *(jahng)(jow-pee-ahn)* **Nà zhāng zhàopiàn duōshao qián? Nà zhāng zhàopiàn** _____ **yuán.**
(M) photo — (M) photo — (34)

21

(jeen-tee-ahn) *(meeng-tee-ahn)* *(zwoh-tee-ahn)*
Jīntiān, Míngtiān, Zuótiān 年
today   tomorrow   yesterday   *nián*

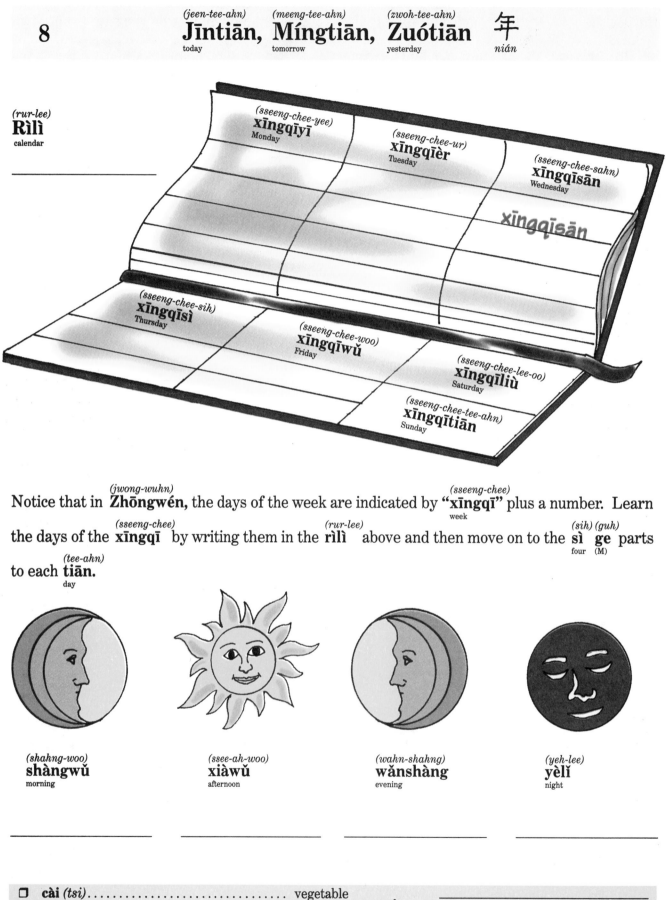

(rur-lee)
Rìlì
calendar

_____

(sseeng-chee-yee)
xīngqīyī
Monday

(sseeng-chee-ur)
xīngqīèr
Tuesday

(sseeng-chee-sahn)
xīngqīsān
Wednesday

xīngqīsān

(sseeng-chee-sih)
xīngqīsì
Thursday

(sseeng-chee-woo)
xīngqīwǔ
Friday

(sseeng-chee-lee-oo)
xīngqīliù
Saturday

(sseeng-chee-tee-ahn)
xīngqītiān
Sunday

(jwong-wuhn) *(sseeng-chee)*
Notice that in **Zhōngwén,** the days of the week are indicated by "**xīngqī**" plus a number. Learn
week

(sseeng-chee) *(rur-lee)* *(sih)* *(guh)*
the days of the **xīngqī** by writing them in the **rìlì** above and then move on to the **sì ge** parts
four (M)

(tee-ahn)
to each **tiān.**
day

(shahng-woo)
shàngwǔ
morning

(ssee-ah-woo)
xiàwǔ
afternoon

(wahn-shahng)
wǎnshàng
evening

(yeh-lee)
yèlǐ
night

_____   _____   _____

☐ **cài** *(tsi)*	vegetable	菜
☐ **báicài** *(by-tsi)*	cabbage	
☐ **bōcài** *(bwoh-tsi)*	spinach	
☐ **qíncài** *(cheen-tsi)*	celery	*cài*
☐ **shēngcài** *(shuhng-tsi)*	lettuce	

It is very important to know the days of the **xīngqī** *(sseeng-chee)* and the various parts of the **tiān** *(tee-ahn)* as well
week   day

as these **sān cí**.

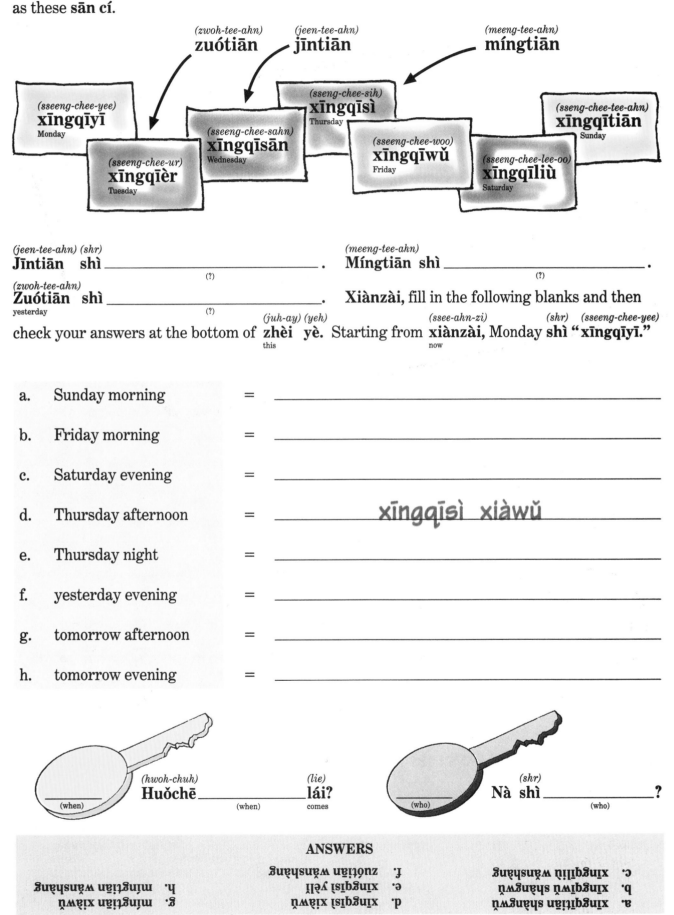

(zwoh-tee-ahn) **zuótiān**   *(jeen-tee-ahn)* **jīntiān**   *(meeng-tee-ahn)* **míngtiān**

(sseeng-chee-yee) **xīngqīyī** Monday

(sseeng-chee-ur) **xīngqīèr** Tuesday

(sseeng-chee-sahn) **xīngqīsān** Wednesday

(sseng-chee-sih) **xīngqīsì** Thursday

(sseeng-chee-woo) **xīngqīwǔ** Friday

(sseeng-chee-lee-oo) **xīngqīliù** Saturday

(sseeng-chee-tee-ahn) **xīngqītiān** Sunday

(jeen-tee-ahn) (shr)
Jīntiān shì _____ .
(?)

(meeng-tee-ahn)
Míngtiān shì _____ .
(?)

(zwoh-tee-ahn)
Zuótiān shì _____ .
yesterday   (?)

Xiànzài, fill in the following blanks and then

check your answers at the bottom of **zhèi yè**. Starting from **xiànzài,** Monday **shì "xīngqīyī."**
(juh-ay) (yeh)   *(ssee-ahn-zi)*   *(shr) (sseeng-chee-yee)*
this   now

a.   Sunday morning   = _____

b.   Friday morning   = _____

c.   Saturday evening   = _____

d.   Thursday afternoon   = _xīngqīsì xiàwǔ_

e.   Thursday night   = _____

f.   yesterday evening   = _____

g.   tomorrow afternoon   = _____

h.   tomorrow evening   = _____

_____ **Huǒchē** _____ **lái?**
(when)   *(hwoh-chuh)*   (when)   *(lie)* comes

_____ **Nà shì** _____ ?
(who)   *(shr)*   (who)

ANSWERS

a.   **xīngqītiān shàngwǔ**
b.   **xīngqīwǔ shàngwǔ**
c.   **xīngqīliù wǎnshàng**
d.   **xīngqīsì xiàwǔ**
e.   **xīngqīsì yèlǐ**
f.   **zuótiān wǎnshàng**
g.   **míngtiān xiàwǔ**
h.   **míngtiān wǎnshàng**

23

Knowing the parts of the **tiān** *(tee-ahn)* day will help you to learn the various greetings in **Zhōngguó huà.** *(jwong-gwoh)* Chinese language

Practice these every day until your trip.

nín zǎo *(neen) (zow)* _____
good morning

wǎnshàng jiàn *(wahn-shahng) (jee-ahn)* _____
see you in the evening

míngtiān jiàn *(jee-ahn)* _____
see you tomorrow

wǎn ān *(wahn) (ahn)* _____
good night

zàijiàn *(zi-jee-ahn)* _____
good-bye/see you later

Take the next group of labels and stick them on the appropriate **dōngxi** *(dwong-ssee)* things in your **fángzi.** *(fahng-zuh)* house Make sure you attach them to the correct items, as they are only in **Zhōngguó huà.** *(hwah)* How about the bathroom mirror for **wǎnshàng jiàn?** *(wahn-shahng)* Or your alarm clock for **míngtiān jiàn?** Let's not forget,

Nǐ hǎo ma? *(nee) (how) (mah)* _____
you good aren't you / how are you

Now for some "**shì**" *(shr)* yes or "**bù**" *(boo)* no questions –

Are your eyes **lán?** *(lahn)* _____   Are your shoes **kāfēisè?** *(kah-fay-suh)* _____

Is your favorite color **hóng?** *(hohng)* _____   Is today **xīngqīliù?** *(sseeng-chee-lee-oo)* _____

Do you own a **gǒu?** *(goh)* _____   Do you own a **māo?** *(mao)* _____

You are about one-fourth of your way through **zhèi běn shū** *(juh-ay) (buhn) (shoo)* this (M) book and it is a good time to quickly review the **cí** you have learned before doing the crossword puzzle on the next **yè.** *(yeh)* When you do the crossword puzzles in this book, do not worry about the tones, focus on the words first and foremost.

CROSSWORD PUZZLE

The grid contains the answer at 5 across: **m í n g z ì**

ACROSS

4. lamp, light
5. name
6. afternoon
8. theater ticket
10. garden
14. tea
15. brown
16. ten
17. gray
19. we
21. bus
25. flower
27. telephone, telephone call
28. house
29. hotel
33. year
35. water
36. yellow
37. two, second

DOWN

1. bicycle
2. car
3. vegetables
4. how much, how many
5. cat
7. dog
8. new
9. color
11. bank
12. two
13. lavatory
15. living room
17. red
18. today
20. black
22. window
23. number
24. week
26. calendar
30. fountain pen
31. chair
32. book
34. where

☐ **càidān** *(tsi-dahn)* .... menu
☐ **càihuā** *(tsi-hwah)* .... cauliflower
☐ **càiyuán** *(tsi-yoo-ahn)* .... vegetable garden
☐ **càiyóu** *(tsi-yoh)* .... vegetable oil
☐ **càizǐr** *(tsi-zur)* .... vegetable seeds

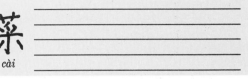

菜
cài

(lee) (shahng) (tswong)
Lǐ, Shàng, Cóng...
inside · on · from

Prepositions in **Zhōngguó huà** *(jwong-gwoh)* (words like "in," "on," "through" and "next to") are easy to
language

learn, and they allow you to be precise with a minimum of effort. Instead of having to point **liù**

times at a piece of yummy snack you would like to purchase, you can explain precisely which one

you want by saying **zài** *(zi)* behind, in front of or under whatever the salesperson is starting to pick
it is

up. Let's learn some of these little **cí**.

(ssee-ah-bee-ahn)
xiàbiān _____
under side (under)

(shahng-bee-ahn)
shàngbiān _____
top   side (over)

(chee-ahn-bee-ahn)
qiánbiān _qiánbiān, qiánbiān_ _____
front   side (in front of)

(pahng-bee-ahn)
pángbiān _____
by   side (next to)

(shahng)
shàng _____
on / on top of

(jeen)
jìn _____
into/in

(lee)
lǐ _____
inside

(hoh-bee-ahn)
hòubiān _____
rear   side (behind)

(tswong)
cóng _____
out of/from

(dee-ahn-sseen)
diǎnxīn _____
snack!

Did you notice that many of these words contain the word **"biān"** *(bee-ahn)* meaning "side"? Fill in the

blanks on the next **yè** *(yeh)* with the correct prepositions.

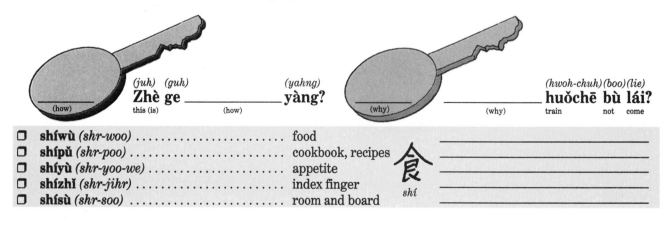

(juh) *(guh)*   *(yahng)*
_____ **Zhè ge** _____ **yàng?**
(how)   this (is)   (how)

(hwoh-chuh)(boo)(lie)
_____ _____ **huǒchē bù lái?**
(why)   (why)   train not come

☐ **shíwù** *(shr-woo)*	food	食 _____
☐ **shípǔ** *(shr-poo)*	cookbook, recipes	*shí* _____
☐ **shíyù** *(shr-yoo-we)*	appetite	_____
☐ **shízhǐ** *(shr-jihr)*	index finger	_____
☐ **shísù** *(shr-soo)*	room and board	_____

Nà diǎnxīn zài zhuōzi _(dee-ahn-sseen) (zi) (jwoh-zuh)_ _____ .
that pastry   is   table   (on)

Nà ge gǒu zài zhuōzi _(goh) (jwoh-zuh)_ _____ .
        dog   table   (under)

Nà ge yīshēng zài nà ge lǚguǎn _(yee-shuhng) (zi) (loo-we-gwahn)_ _____ .
(M) doctor   is   hotel   (inside)

Nà ge yīshēng zài nǎr? _(yee-shuhng)_ _____
that (M)

Nà ge nánrén zài nà ge lǚguǎn _(nahn-ruhn) (loo-we-gwahn)_ _____ .
that (M) man   hotel   (in front of)

Nà ge nánrén zài nǎr? _____

Nà ge diànhuà zài huàr _(dee-ahn-hwah) (hwahr)_ _____ .
telephone   picture   (next to)

Nà ge diànhuà zài nǎr? _____

Xiànzài, _(ssee-ahn-zi)_ fill in each blank on the picture below with the best possible one of these little **cí.**
now

Hopefully you will enjoy many Chinese gardens similar to the one below.

(over)

(behind)

(next to)

(in front of)

(in, into)

(under)

☐	**guó** (_gwoh_)	nation, state	
☐	**Fǎguó** (_fah-gwoh_)	France	
☐	**Měiguó** (_may-gwoh_)	United States	王.
☐	**Yīngguó** (_yeeng-gwoh_)	England	_guó_
☐	**Zhōngguó** (_jwong-gwoh_)	China	

(yee-yoo-eh) *(ur-yoo-eh)* *(sahn-yoo-eh)*

Yīyuè, Èryuè, Sānyuè
January   February   March

You have learned the days of the *(sseeng-chee)* **xīngqī,** so *(ssee-ahn-zi)* **xiànzài** it is time to learn the *(yoo-eh)* **yuè** of the *(nee-ahn)* **nián** and
week   now   months   year

all the different kinds of *(tee-ahn-chee)* **tiānqì.**
weather

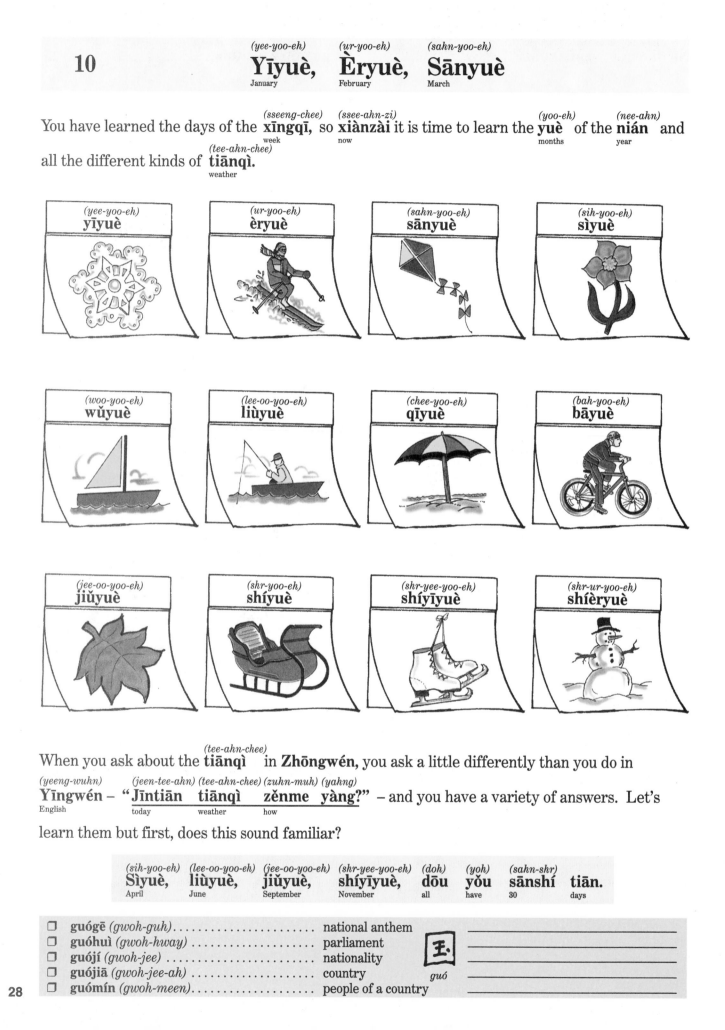

(yee-yoo-eh) **yīyuè**

(ur-yoo-eh) **èryuè**

(sahn-yoo-eh) **sānyuè**

(sih-yoo-eh) **sìyuè**

(woo-yoo-eh) **wǔyuè**

(lee-oo-yoo-eh) **liùyuè**

(chee-yoo-eh) **qīyuè**

(bah-yoo-eh) **bāyuè**

(jee-oo-yoo-eh) **jiǔyuè**

(shr-yoo-eh) **shíyuè**

(shr-yee-yoo-eh) **shíyīyuè**

(shr-ur-yoo-eh) **shíèryuè**

When you ask about the *(tee-ahn-chee)* **tiānqì** in **Zhōngwén,** you ask a little differently than you do in
(yeeng-wuhn) *(jeen-tee-ahn)* *(tee-ahn-chee)* *(zuhn-muh)* *(yahng)*
Yīngwén – "**Jīntiān tiānqì zěnme yàng?**" – and you have a variety of answers. Let's
English   today   weather   how

learn them but first, does this sound familiar?

| *(sih-yoo-eh)* **Sìyuè,** April | *(lee-oo-yoo-eh)* **liùyuè,** June | *(jee-oo-yoo-eh)* **jiǔyuè,** September | *(shr-yee-yoo-eh)* **shíyīyuè,** November | *(doh)* **dōu** all | *(yoh)* **yǒu** have | *(sahn-shr)* **sānshí** 30 | **tiān.** days |

- [ ] **guógē** *(gwoh-guh)* . . . . national anthem
- [ ] **guóhuì** *(gwoh-hway)* . . . . parliament
- [ ] **guójí** *(gwoh-jee)* . . . . nationality
- [ ] **guójiā** *(gwoh-jee-ah)* . . . . country
- [ ] **guómín** *(gwoh-meen)* . . . . people of a country

王. *guó*

(jeen-tee-ahn) (tee-ahn-chee) (zuhn-muh) (yahng)
Jīntiān tiānqì zěnme yàng? _____
today   weather   how   kind

(yee-yoo-eh) (ssee-ah-ssee-yoo-eh)
Yīyuè xiàxuě. _____
        (it) snows

(ur-yoo-eh) (yuh) (ssee-ah-ssee-yoo-eh)
Èryuè yě xiàxuě. _____
    also

(ssee-ah-yoo-we)
Sānyuè xiàyǔ. _____
    rains

(sih-yoo-eh) (ssee-ah-yoo-we)
Sìyuè yě xiàyǔ. _____
    also rains

(gwah-fung)
Wǔyuè guāfēng. _____
    windy

(lee-oo-yoo-eh) (yuh) (gwah-fung)
Liùyuè yě guāfēng. _____

(chee-yoo-eh) (huhn) (noo-ahn-hwoh)
Qīyuè hěn nuǎnhuo. _____
    very warm

(bah-yoo-eh) (huhn) (ruh)
Bāyuè hěn rè. _____
    very   hot

(jee-oo-yoo-eh) (tee-ahn-chee) (how)
Jiǔyuè tiānqì hǎo. _____
    weather   good

(shr-yoo-eh) (tee-ahn-chee) (chahng-chahng) (how)
Shíyuè tiānqì chángcháng hǎo. _____
           usually

(shr-yee-yoo-eh) (huhn) (lung)
Shíyīyuè hěn lěng. _____
    very cold

(shr-ur-yoo-eh) (tee-ahn-chee) (boo)(how)
Shíèryuè tiānqì hěn bù hǎo. _____
    weather very not good

(ur-yoo-eh) (yahng)
Èryuè tiānqì zěnme yàng? _____
    weather how   kind

(sih-yoo-eh)
Sìyuè tiānqì zěnme yàng? *Sìyuè xiàyǔ. Sìyuè xiàyǔ. Sìyuè xiàyǔ.*
April   how   kind

(woo-yoo-eh)
Wǔyuè tiānqì zěnme yàng? _____

(bah-yoo-eh)
Bāyuè tiānqì zěnme yàng? _____

❏ **guónèi** *(gwoh-nay)*	domestic		_____
❏ **guóqí** *(gwoh-chee)*	national flag		_____
❏ **guówài** *(gwoh-why)*	overseas	王	_____
❏ **guówáng** *(gwoh-wahng)*	king	*guó*	_____
❏ **guóyíng** *(gwoh-yeeng)*	state-owned		_____

29

Xiànzài for the seasons of the *(nee-ahn)* **nián** . . .
year

(dwong-tee-ahn)
dōngtiān
winter

(ssee-ah-tee-ahn)
xiàtiān
summer

(chee-yoo-tee-ahn)
qiūtiān
autumn

(choon-tee-ahn)
chūntiān
spring

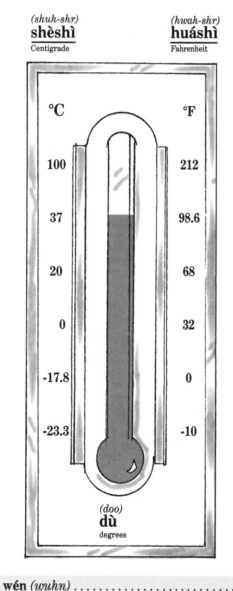

(shuh-shr)
shèshì
Centigrade

(hwah-shr)
huáshì
Fahrenheit

°C	°F
100	212
37	98.6
20	68
0	32
-17.8	0
-23.3	-10

(doo)
dù
degrees

At this point, it is a good time to familiarize yourself with **Zhōngguó** *(chee-wuhn)* **qìwēn.** Carefully study the *temperatures* thermometer because temperatures in **Zhōngguó** are calculated on the basis of Centigrade (not Fahrenheit).

To convert °F to °C, subtract 32 and multiply by 0.55.

98.6 °F - 32 = 66.6 x 0.55 = 37 °C

To convert °C to °F, multiply by 1.8 and add 32.

37 °C x 1.8 = 66.6 + 32 = 98.6 °F

What is normal body temperature in *(shuh-shr)* **shèshì?**

What is the freezing point in **shèshì?**

☐ **wén** *(wuhn)*	written language	
☐ **Déwén** *(duh-wuhn)*	German	文
☐ **Fǎwén** *(fah-wuhn)*	French	
☐ **Yīngwén** *(yeeng-wuhn)*	English	
☐ **Zhōngwén** *(jwong-wuhn)*	Chinese	*wén*

(jee-ah)   *(jee-ah-teeng)*
Jiā – Jiātíng
home   family

Study the family tree below. Notice that, in **Zhōngguó,** the family name comes first, and the given name (or what we, in **Měiguó,** *(may-gwoh)* / America / think of as the first name) follows. Also, women keep their given or maiden name when they marry.

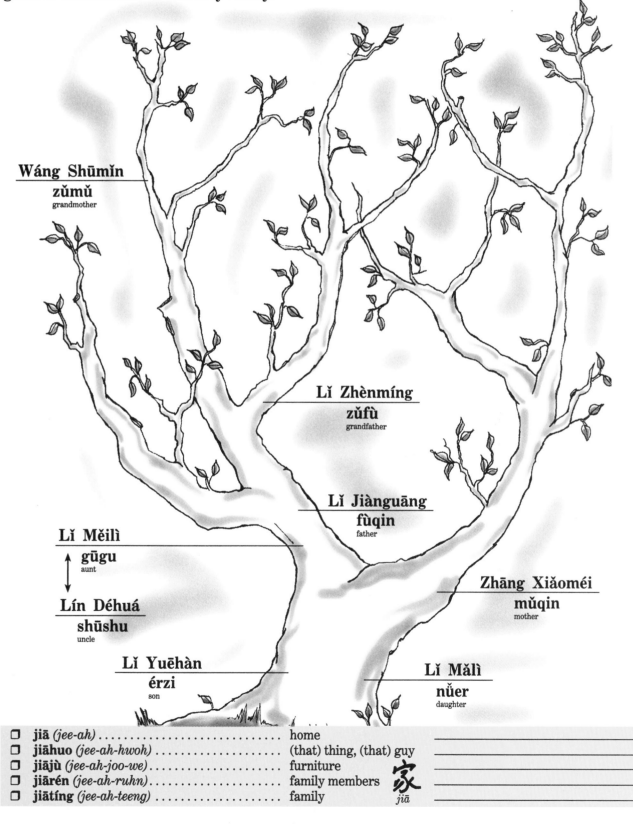

Wáng Shūmǐn
zǔmǔ
grandmother

Lǐ Zhènmíng
zǔfù
grandfather

Lǐ Jiànguāng
fùqin
father

Lǐ Měilì
gūgu
aunt

Lín Déhuá
shūshu
uncle

Zhāng Xiǎoméi
mǔqin
mother

Lǐ Yuēhàn
érzi
son

Lǐ Mǎlì
nǚer
daughter

☐ **jiā** *(jee-ah)*	home	_____
☐ **jiāhuo** *(jee-ah-hwoh)*	(that) thing, (that) guy	_____
☐ **jiājù** *(jee-ah-joo-we)*	furniture	_____
☐ **jiārén** *(jee-ah-ruhn)*	family members	_____
☐ **jiātíng** *(jee-ah-teeng)*	family	_____

家
jiā

Let's learn **zěnme** to identify family members by **míngzì**. Study the following examples carefully.
how _(meeng-zuh)_ _name_

(nee) (jee-ow) _(meeng-zuh)_
Nǐ jiào shénme míngzì?_____
you _called_ _what_ _name_

(woh)
Wǒ jiào _____.
_I_ _called_ _(your name)_

(foo-moo)
fùmǔ
parents

(foo-cheen)
fùqin _____
father

(foo-cheen) (jee-ow) _(meeng-zuh)_
Fùqin jiào shénme míngzì?_____
father _called_ _what_ _name_

(moo-cheen)
mǔqin _____
mother

(moo-cheen)
Mǔqin jiào shénme míngzì?_____
father _called_ _what_ _name_

(ssee-ow-hi)
xiǎohái
children

(ur-zuh) _(noo-we-ur)_ _(guh-guh)_ _(may-may)_
Érzi and **nǚér** are also **gēge** and **mèimei**
(older) brother _(younger) sister_

to each other.

(ur-zuh)
érzi _____
son

(ur-zuh) (jee-ow)
Érzi jiào shénme míngzì?_____
son _called_ _what_ _name_

(noo-we-ur)
nǚér _____
daughter

(noo-we-ur)
Nǚér jiào shénme míngzì?_____
daughter _called_ _what_ _name_

(zoo-foo-moo)
zǔfùmǔ
grandparents

(zoo-foo)
zǔfù _____
grandfather

(zoo-foo)
Zǔfù jiào shénme míngzì?_____
grandfather

(zoo-moo)
zǔmǔ _____
grandmother

(zoo-moo)
Zǔmǔ jiào shénme míngzì?_____

Now you ask —

_____
(How are you called?/What is your name?)

And answer —

_____
(My name is . . .)

☐ **shuǐ** _(shway)_	. . . .	water	
☐ **shuǐchē** _(shway-chuh)_	. . . .	watermill	
☐ **shuǐchí** _(shway-chr)_	. . . .	pool	水 _____
☐ **shuǐfèn** _(shway-fuhn)_	. . . .	moisture	_shuǐ_
☐ **shuǐpíng** _(shway-peeng)_	. . . .	water bottle	

(choo-fahng)
Chúfáng
kitchen

(beeng-ssee-ahng)
bīngxiāng
refrigerator

_____

(loo-zuh)
lúzi
stove

_____

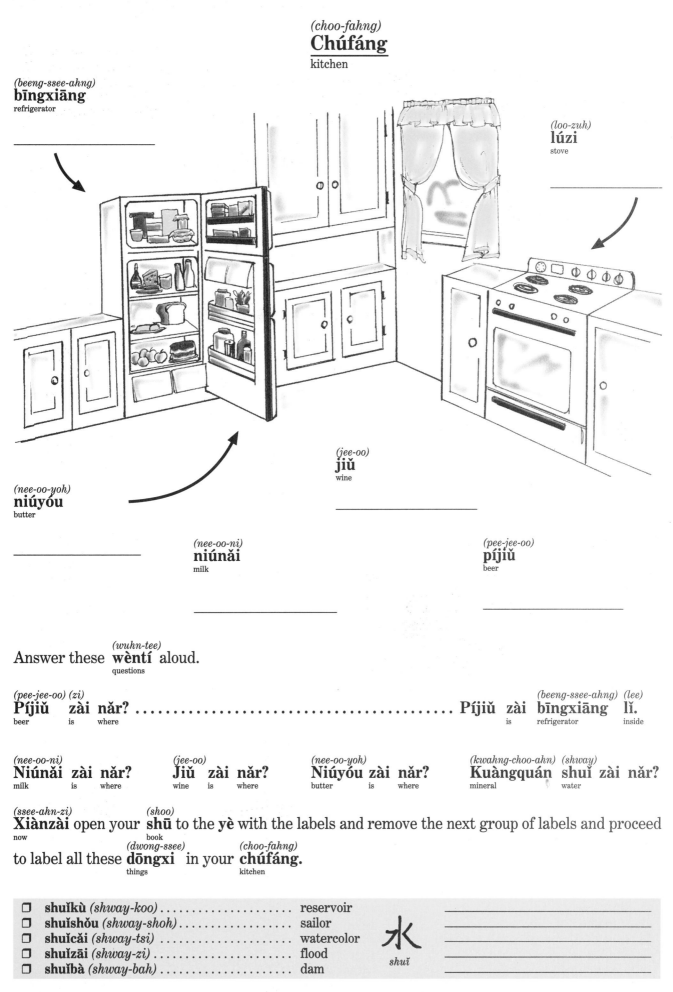

(jee-oo)
jiǔ
wine

_____

(nee-oo-yoh)
niúyóu
butter

_____

(nee-oo-ni)
niúnǎi
milk

_____

(pee-jee-oo)
píjiǔ
beer

_____

Answer these *(wuhn-tee)* **wèntí** aloud.
questions

(pee-jee-oo) *(zi)*
Píjiǔ zài nǎr? . . . . **Píjiǔ zài bīngxiāng lǐ.**
beer   is   where   is   refrigerator   inside

(nee-oo-ni)
Niúnǎi zài nǎr?
milk   is   where

(jee-oo)
Jiǔ zài nǎr?
wine   is   where

(nee-oo-yoh)
Niúyóu zài nǎr?
butter is   where

(kwahng-choo-ahn) *(shway)*
Kuàngquán shuǐ zài nǎr?
mineral   water

(ssee-ahn-zi) *(shoo)*
Xiànzài open your **shū** to the **yè** with the labels and remove the next group of labels and proceed
now   book

(dwong-ssee) *(choo-fahng)*
to label all these **dōngxi** in your **chúfáng.**
things   kitchen

❏	**shuǐkù** *(shway-koo)*	reservoir		_____
❏	**shuǐshǒu** *(shway-shoh)*	sailor		_____
❏	**shuǐcǎi** *(shway-tsi)*	watercolor	水	_____
❏	**shuǐzāi** *(shway-zi)*	flood	*shuǐ*	_____
❏	**shuǐbà** *(shway-bah)*	dam		_____

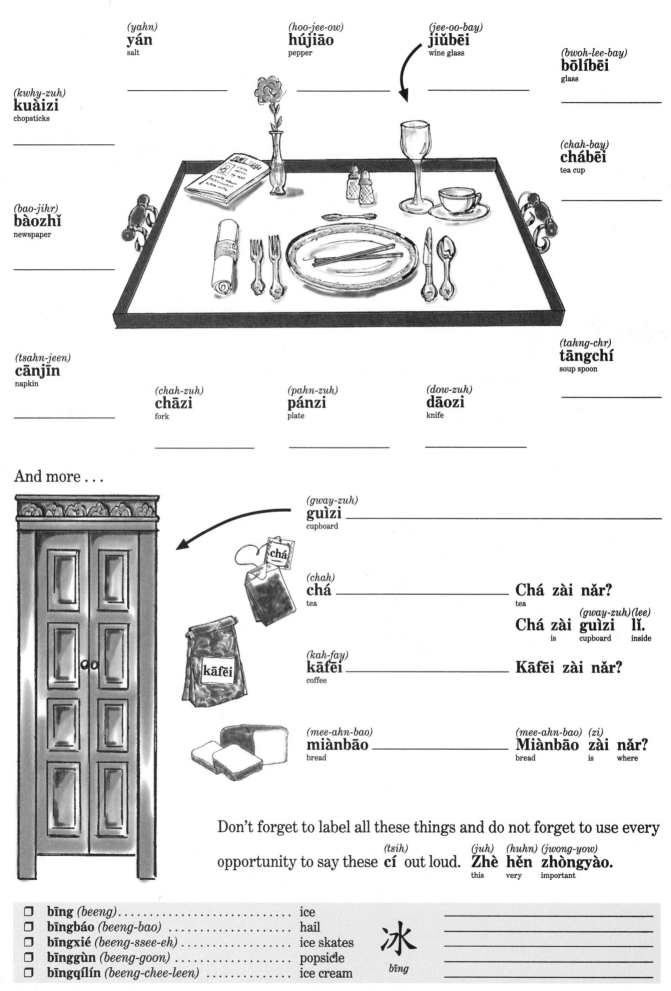

(yahn)
yán
salt

(hoo-jee-ow)
hújiāo
pepper

(jee-oo-bay)
jiǔbēi
wine glass

(bwoh-lee-bay)
bōlíbēi
glass

(kwhy-zuh)
kuàizi
chopsticks

(chah-bay)
chábēi
tea cup

(bao-jihr)
bàozhǐ
newspaper

(tsahn-jeen)
cānjīn
napkin

(tahng-chr)
tāngchí
soup spoon

(chah-zuh)
chāzi
fork

(pahn-zuh)
pánzi
plate

(dow-zuh)
dāozi
knife

And more . . .

(gway-zuh)
guìzi
cupboard

(chah)
chá
tea

Chá zài nǎr?
tea

(gway-zuh)(lee)
Chá zài guìzi lǐ.
is   cupboard   inside

(kah-fay)
kāfēi
coffee

Kāfēi zài nǎr?

(mee-ahn-bao)
miànbāo
bread

(mee-ahn-bao) (zi)
Miànbāo zài nǎr?
bread   is   where

Don't forget to label all these things and do not forget to use every

opportunity to say these *(tsih)* **cí** out loud.   *(juh) (huhn) (jwong-yow)*
Zhè hěn zhòngyào.
this   very   important

☐ **bīng** *(beeng)* . . . . ice
☐ **bīngbáo** *(beeng-bao)* . . . . hail
☐ **bīngxié** *(beeng-ssee-eh)* . . . . ice skates   冰
☐ **bīnggùn** *(beeng-goon)* . . . . popsicle   *bīng*
34   ☐ **bīngqílín** *(beeng-chee-leen)* . . . . ice cream

(ssee-eh-ssee-eh) **xièxie**	*(shoo)* **shū**	*(gwah-lee-ahn-dow)* **guāliǎndāo**	*(nee-oo-zi-koo)* **niúzǎikù**
(dway-boo-chee) **duìbùqǐ**	*(sseen)* **xìn**	*(choo-hahn-jee)* **chúhànjì**	*(dwahn-koo)* **duǎnkù**
(yee-choo) **yīchú**	*(yoh-pee-ow)* **yóupiào**	*(shoo-zuh)* **shūzi**	*(wuhn-hwah-shahn)* **wénhuàshān**
(chwahng) **chuáng**	*(meeng-sseen-pee-ahn)* **míngxìnpiàn**	*(yoo-we-yee)* **yǔyī**	*(nay-koo)* **nèikù**
(juhn-toh) **zhěntóu**	*(hoo-jow)* **hùzhào**	*(sahn)* **sǎn**	*(nay-yee)* **nèiyī**
(bay-zuh) **bèizi**	*(fay-jee-pee-ow)* **fēijīpiào**	*(dah-yee)* **dàyī**	*(lee-ahn-yee-choon)* **liányīqún**
(now-jwong) **nàozhōng**	*(ssee-ahng-zuh)* **xiāngzi**	*(shoh-tao)* **shǒutào**	*(chuhn-yee)* **chènyī**
(jeeng-zuh) **jìngzi**	*(pee-bao)* **píbāo**	*(mao-zuh)* **màozi**	*(choon-zuh)* **qúnzi**
(ssee-lee-ahn-puhn) **xǐliǎnpén**	*(pee-jee-ah-zuh)* **píjiāzi**	*(ssee-yoo-eh-zuh)* **xuēzi**	*(mao-yee)* **máoyī**
(mao-jeen) **máojīn**	*(chee-ahn)* **qián**	*(ssee-eh)* **xié**	*(chuhn-choon)* **chènqún**
(mah-twong) **mǎtǒng**	*(sseen-yohng-kah)* **xìnyòngkǎ**	*(yoon-dohng-ssee-eh)* **yùndòngxié**	*(ssee-wong-jow)* **xiōngzhào**
(leen-yoo-we) **línyù**	*(loo-we-sseng) (jihr-pee-ow)* **lǚxíng zhīpiào**	*(ssee-jwahng)* **xīzhuāng**	*(wah-zuh)* **wàzi**
(chee-ahn-bee) **qiānbǐ**	*(jow-ssee-ahng-jee)* **zhàoxiàngjī**	*(leeng-die)* **lǐngdài**	*(koo-wah)* **kùwà**
(gahng-bee) **gāngbǐ**	*(jee-ow-joo-ahn)* **jiāojuǎn**	*(chuhn-yee)* **chènyī**	*(shway-yee)* **shuìyī**
(dee-ahn-shr) **diànshì**	*(yoh-yohng-yee)* **yóuyǒngyī**	*(shoh-joo-ahn)* **shǒujuàn**	*(shway-yee)* **shuìyī**
(dee-ahn-now) **diànnǎo**	*(lee-ahng-ssee-eh)* **liángxié**	*(why-tao)* **wàitào**	*(shway-pow)* **shuìpáo**
(jihr) **zhǐ**	*(tie-yahng) (yahn-jeeng)* **tàiyáng yǎnjìng**	*(koo-zuh)* **kùzi**	*(twoh-ssee-eh)* **tuōxié**
(yahn-jeeng) **yǎnjìng**	*(yah-shwah)* **yáshuā**	*(woh) (tswong) (may-gwoh) (lie)* **Wǒ cóng Měiguó lái.**	
(zah-jihr) **zázhì**	*(yah-gow)* **yágāo**	*(woh) (ssee-ahng) (ssee-yoo-eh-ssee) (jwong-wuhn)* **Wǒ xiǎng xuéxí Zhōngwén.**	
(zih-jihr-loh) **zìzhǐlǒu**	*(fay-zow)* **féizào**	*(woh) (jee-ow)* **Wǒ jiào _____ .**	

PLUS ...

This book includes a number of other innovative features unique to the *"10 minutes a day®"* Series. At the back of this book, you will find twelve pages of flash cards. Cut them out and flip through them at least once a day.

On pages 116, 117 and 118 you will find a beverage guide and a menu guide. Don't wait until your trip to use them. Clip out the menu guide and use it tonight at the dinner table. Take them both with you the next time you dine at your favorite Chinese restaurant.

By using the special features in this book, you will be speaking Chinese before you know it.

(yee) (loo) (peeng) (ahn)
Yí lù píng ān!
safe and peaceful journey

(zwong-jee-ow)
Zōngjiào
religion

In **Zhōngguó**, there is not the wide variety of *(zwong-jee-ow)* **zōngjiào** that **wǒmen** find in *(may-gwoh)* **Měiguó.** In
we ⁣ ⁣ ⁣ ⁣ ⁣ ⁣ ⁣ ⁣America

Zhōngguó, a person's *(zwong-jee-ow)* **zōngjiào** *(chahng-chahng)* **chángcháng** *(shr)* **shì** one of the following.
religion ⁣ ⁣ ⁣generally ⁣ ⁣ ⁣ ⁣is

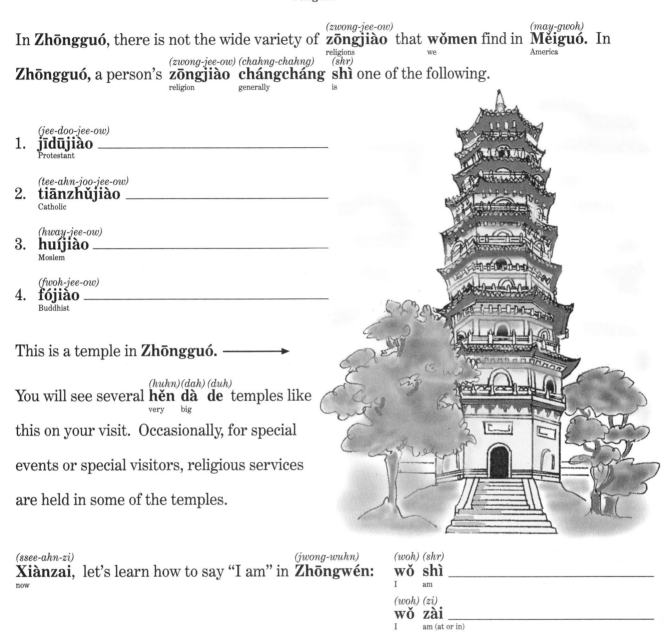

(jee-doo-jee-ow)
1. **jīdūjiào** _____
Protestant

(tee-ahn-joo-jee-ow)
2. **tiānzhǔjiào** _____
Catholic

(hway-jee-ow)
3. **huíjiào** _____
Moslem

(fwoh-jee-ow)
4. **fójiào** _____
Buddhist

This is a temple in **Zhōngguó.** ⟶

(huhn)(dah)(duh)
You will see several **hěn dà de** temples like
very ⁣ ⁣big

this on your visit. Occasionally, for special

events or special visitors, religious services

are held in some of the temples.

(ssee-ahn-zi)
Xiànzai, let's learn how to say "I am" in **Zhōngwén:** *(jwong-wuhn)*
now

(woh) (shr)
wǒ shì _____
I ⁣ ⁣am

(woh) (zi)
wǒ zài _____
I ⁣ ⁣am (at or in)

(huhn)
Both these forms should look **hěn** familiar. You have been using them since Step 2! Test yourself –

write each sentence on the next page for more practice. Add your own variations as well.

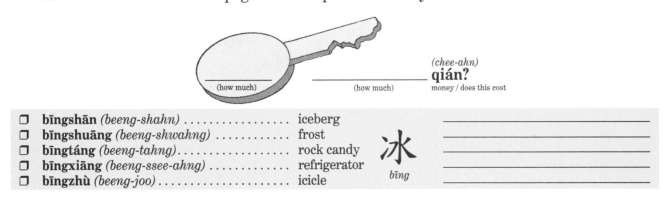

_____ _____ *(chee-ahn)* **qián?**
(how much) ⁣ ⁣ ⁣ ⁣(how much) ⁣ ⁣ ⁣ ⁣money / does this cost

❏ **bīngshān** *(beeng-shahn)*	iceberg		_____
❏ **bīngshuāng** *(beeng-shwahng)*	frost	冰	_____
❏ **bīngtáng** *(beeng-tahng)*	rock candy		_____
❏ **bīngxiāng** *(beeng-ssee-ahng)*	refrigerator		_____
❏ **bīngzhù** *(beeng-joo)*	icicle	*bīng*	_____

Wǒ *(shr)* **shì** *(fwoh-jee-ow)* **fójiào** *(too)* **tú.** _____
I · am · Buddhist · disciple

Wǒ *(zi)* **zài** *(jwong-gwoh)* **Zhōngguó.** _____
am (in) China

Wǒ *(shr)* **shì** *(hway-jee-ow)* **huíjiào** *(too)* **tú.** _____
Moslem · disciple

Wǒ **zài** *(oh-joh)* **Ōuzhōu.** _____
am · Europe

Wǒ **shì** *(jee-doo-jee-ow)* **jīdūjiào** *(too)* **tú.** _____
Protestant · disciple

Wǒ **zài** *(loo-we-gwahn)* **lǚguǎn** *(lee)* **lǐ.** _____
hotel · inside

Wǒ **shì** *(tee-ahn-joo-jee-ow)* **tiānzhǔjiào** **tú.** _____
Catholic · disciple

Wǒ **zài** *(yeen-hahng)* **yínháng** *(lee)* **lǐ.** _____
bank · inside

Wǒ **shì** *(yeeng-gwoh)* **Yīngguó** *(ruhn)* **rén.** _____
British · person

Wǒ **zài** *(choo-fahng)* **chúfáng** *(lee)* **lǐ.** _____
kitchen · inside

Wǒ **shì** *(jee-ah-nah-dah)* **Jiānádà** *(ruhn)* **rén.** _____
Canadian · person

Wǒ **zài** *(fahn-gwahn)* **fànguǎn** *(lee)* **lǐ.** _____
inside

Wǒ **shì** *(may-gwoh)* **Měiguó** *(ruhn)* **rén.** _____
American · person

Wǒ **zài** *(fahng-zuh)* **fángzi** *(lee)* **lǐ.** _____
inside

To negate any of these statements, simply add "**bù**" *(boo)* after the subject.
not/no

Wǒ *(boo)* **bù** *(shr)* **shì** *(fwoh-jee-ow)* **fójiào** *(too)* **tú.** _____
I · not · am · Buddhist · disciple

Wǒ *(boo)* **bù** *(zi)* **zài** *(jwong-gwoh)* **Zhōngguó.** _____
not · am (in) China

Go through and drill these sentences again but with "**bù.**"

Xiànzài, *(ssee-ahn-zi)* take a piece of paper. Our **jiātíng** *(jee-ah-teeng)* from earlier had a reunion. Identify everyone
family

below by writing the **zhěngquède** *(jung-choo-eh-duh)* **Zhōngwén cí** for each **rén** *(ruhn)* – **mǔqin, shūshu,** and so on.
correct · person

Don't forget the **gǒu!** *(goh)*

❑	**fēi** *(fay)*	to fly	
❑	**fēijī** *(fay-jee)*	airplane	
❑	**fēijīchǎng** *(fay-jee-chahng)*	airport	
❑	**fēijīkù** *(fay-jee-koo)*	hangar	
❑	**fēiqín** *(fay-cheen)*	birds	

fēi

(ssee-yoo-eh-ssee)
Xuéxí!
to learn

You have already used two very important verbs: **wǒ** *(ssee-ahng)* **xiǎng** *(yow)* **yào** and **wǒ** *(yoh)* **yǒu.** Although you
I   would like   I   have

might be able to get by with only these verbs, let's assume you want to do better. First a quick review.

How do you say   "I"   in **Zhōngwén?** _____

How do you say   "we"   in **Zhōngwén?** _____

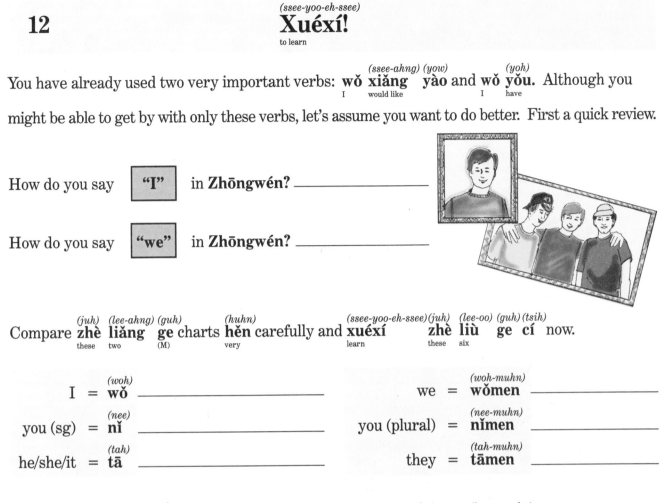

(juh) *(lee-ahng)* *(guh)* *(huhn)* *(ssee-yoo-eh-ssee)* *(juh)* *(lee-oo)* *(guh)* *(tsih)*
Compare **zhè liǎng ge** charts **hěn** carefully and **xuéxí zhè liù ge cí** now.
these two (M) very learn these six

I = **wǒ** *(woh)* _____   we = **wǒmen** *(woh-muhn)* _____

you (sg) = **nǐ** *(nee)* _____   you (plural) = **nǐmen** *(nee-muhn)* _____

he/she/it = **tā** *(tah)* _____   they = **tāmen** *(tah-muhn)* _____

(yeeng-wuhn) *(jwong-wuhn)*
Not too hard, is it? Draw lines between the matching **Yīngwén** and **Zhōngwén cí** below to see
English Chinese

if you can keep these **cí** straight in your mind.

(woh-muhn)
wǒmen   I

(nee-muhn)
nǐmen   they

(tah)
tā   you (plural)

(woh)
wǒ   he

(nee)
nǐ   we

(tah)
tā   she

(tah-muhn)
tāmen   you (singular)

❏	**fēisù** *(fay-soo)*	quickly
❏	**fēiwǔ** *(fay-woo)*	to flutter
❏	**fēixíng** *(fay-sseeng)*	to soar
❏	**fēixíngyuán** *(fay-sseeng-yoo-ahn)*	pilot
❏	**fēiyú** *(fay-yoo-we)*	flying fish

飞
fēi

_____
_____
_____
_____
_____

Xiànzài *(ssee-ahn-zi)* close this **shū** and write out both columns of the above exercise on a piece of **zhǐ** *(jihr)* and do it again. How did **nǐ** do? **Hǎo** *(how)* good or **bù hǎo?** *(boo)(how)* not good **Mǎmǎhūhū?** *(mah-mah-hoo-hoo)* so so **Xiànzài** that **nǐ** *(nee)* you know these **cí, nǐ** can

say almost anything in **Zhōngwén** with one basic formula: the "plug-in" formula.

To demonstrate, let's take **liù** *(lee-oo)* six **ge** (M) basic and practical verbs and see how the "plug-in" formula works. Write the verbs in the blanks after **nǐ** *(nee)* you have practiced saying them out loud many times.

lái *(lie)* to come _____

xuéxí *(ssee-yoo-eh-ssee)* to learn _____

qù *(chee-oo)* to go (to) qù, qù, qù, qù, qù, qù

yǒu *(yoh)* to have _____

xiǎng yào *(ssee-ahng) (yow)* would like _____

xūyào *(ssee-oo-yow)* to need _____

Besides the familiar words already circled, can **nǐ** find the above verbs in the puzzle below?

When **nǐ** find them, write them in the blanks to the right.

P	D	O	Q	Ù	A	I	D	E	À	X
A	U	C	N	P	C	N	Ǎ	R	E	U
E	Ō	X	Ū	Y	À	O	J	J	Í	É
W	S	L	S	J	E	E	U	O	I	X
E	H	Á	E	Ǐ	T	Z	U	Y	E	Í
J	A	I	I	I	E	Ó	M	Ǒ	W	E
D	O	N	Z	H	X	B	D	U	I	F
X	I	Ǎ	N	G	Y	À	O	Y	Ǐ	È

1. _____

2. _____

3. _____

4. _____

5. _____

6. _____

Study the following patterns carefully.

wǒ	*(lie)* **lái**	=	I *come*
nǐ	**lái**	=	you *come*
tā	**lái**	=	he, she or it *comes*
wǒmen	**lái**	=	we *come*
nǐmen	**lái**	=	you *come*
tāmen	**lái**	=	they *come*

wǒ	*(chee-oo)* **qù**	=	I *go*
nǐ	**qù**	=	you *go*
tā	**qù**	=	he, she or it *goes*
wǒmen	**qù**	=	we *go*
nǐmen	**qù**	=	you *go*
tāmen	**qù**	=	they *go*

Note: • Regardless of the subject of the sentence in Chinese (I, we, you, he, she, it, they), the same verb form is used. Verbs remain the same in Chinese – they do not have different endings. What could be easier?

Notice that **"men"** *(muhn)* is added to a word to indicate more than one person.

wǒ	=	I	*(woh-muhn)* **wǒmen**	=	we
(nee) **nǐ**	=	you (singular)	*(nee-muhn)* **nǐmen**	=	you (plural as in "you all")
tā	=	he, she or it	*(tah-muhn)* **tāmen**	=	they

Note: • Unlike English, the same word is used for he, she and it: **tā.**

he *learns* she *learns* it *learns*	**tā xuéxí** *(ssee-yoo-eh-ssee)* _____

he *would like* she *would like* it *would like*	**tā xiǎng yào** *(ssee-ahng) (yow)* _____

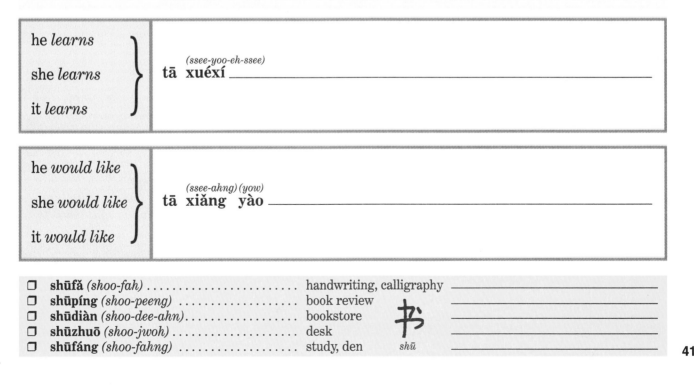

☐ **shūfǎ** *(shoo-fah)* . . . . handwriting, calligraphy _____
☐ **shūpíng** *(shoo-peeng)* . . . . book review _____
☐ **shūdiàn** *(shoo-dee-ahn)* . . . . bookstore _____
☐ **shūzhuō** *(shoo-jwoh)* . . . . desk _____
☐ **shūfáng** *(shoo-fahng)* . . . . study, den *shū* _____

Here's your next group!

	(yoh)		
wǒ	yǒu	=	I *have*
nǐ	yǒu	=	you *have*
tā	yǒu	=	he, she or it *has*
wǒmen	yǒu	=	we *have*
nǐmen	yǒu	=	you *have*
tāmen	yǒu	=	they *have*

	(ssee-oo-yow)		
wǒ	xūyào	=	I *need*
nǐ	xūyào	=	you *need*
tā	xūyào	=	he, she or it *needs*
wǒmen	xūyào	=	we *need*
nǐmen	xūyào	=	you *need*
tāmen	xūyào	=	they *need*

In **Zhōngwén**, **dòngcí** *(dwong-tsih)* are easy to learn. **Zhèr** *(juhr)* **yǒu** *(yoh)* **liù** *(lee-oo)* **ge dòngcí.** *(dwong-tsih)*
verbs — here — six — — verbs

(jee-ow)
jiào _____
to be called, named

(my)
mǎi _____
to buy

(shwoh)
shuō _____
to speak

(joo)
zhù _____
to live, reside

(jee-ow)
jiào _____
to order

(teeng-lee-oo)
tíngliú _____
to stay

Notice that the verb for "to order" and "to be called" is one and the same: **Jiào.** *(jee-ow)* Don't panic or

give up. Just think of it as one less word to learn. Be sure to write out all these verbs and

sentences and then try to use them in sentences of your own.

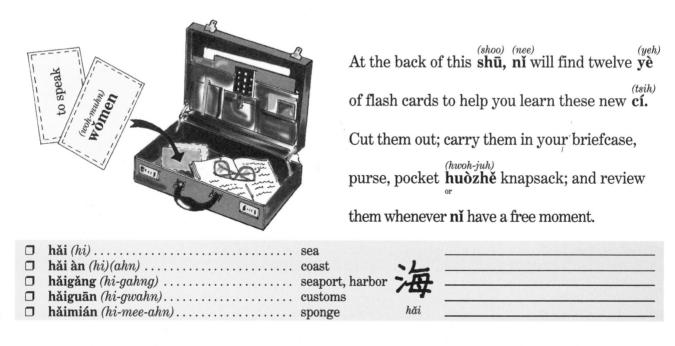

At the back of this **shū** *(shoo)*, **nǐ** *(nee)* will find twelve **yè** *(yeh)*

of flash cards to help you learn these new **cí.** *(tsih)*

Cut them out; carry them in your briefcase,

purse, pocket **huòzhě** *(hwoh-juh)* knapsack; and review
or

them whenever **nǐ** have a free moment.

❐ **hǎi** *(hi)*	sea		_____
❐ **hǎi àn** *(hi)(ahn)*	coast		_____
❐ **hǎigǎng** *(hi-gahng)*	seaport, harbor	海	_____
❐ **hǎiguān** *(hi-gwahn)*	customs		_____
❐ **hǎimián** *(hi-mee-ahn)*	sponge	*hǎi*	_____

(ssee-ahn-zi)
Xiànzài, it is your turn to practice what **nǐ** *(nee)* have learned. Fill in the following blanks with the

correct form of the **dòngcí.** *(dwong-tsih)* Each time **nǐ** write out the sentence, be sure to say it aloud.
verb

(lie)
lái
to come

Wǒ cóng Měiguó _____ .
from   America

Nǐ cóng Déguó _____ .
Germany

Tā cóng Fǎguó _lái/_____ .
France

Wǒmen cóng Yīngguó _____ .
England

Tāmen cóng Zhōngguó _____ .

(ssee-yoo-eh-ssee)
xuéxi
to learn

Wǒ _____ **Zhōngwén.** *(jwong-wuhn)*

Nǐ _____ **Yīngwén.** *(yeeng-wuhn)*
English

Tā _____ **Zhōngwén.**

Wǒmen _____ **Yīngwén.**

Tāmen _____ **Zhōngwén.**

(chee-oo)
qù
to go (to)

Wǒ _____ **Déguó.** *(duh-gwoh)*
Germany

Nǐ _____ **Fǎguó.** *(fah-gwoh)*
France

Tā _qù/_____ **Yìdàlì.** *(yee-dah-lee)*
Italy

Wǒmen _____ **Hélán.** *(huh-lahn)*
Netherlands

Tāmen _____ **Zhōngguó.**

(yoh)
yǒu
to have

Wǒ _____ **wǔ yuán.** *(woo)*
five yuan

Nǐ _____ **liù yuán.** *(lee-oo)*
six

Tā _____ **bā yuán.**

Wǒmen _____ **shí yuán.** *(shr)*
ten

Tāmen _____ **sān yuán.**

(ssee-ahng) (yow)
xiǎng yào
would like

Wǒ _____ **yì bēi jiǔ.** *(yee) (bay) (jee-oo)*
one cup/glass wine

Nǐ _____ **yì bēi chá.** *(chah)*
cup   tea

Tā _____ **yì bēi shuǐ.** *(shway)*
(M)   water

Wǒmen _____ **yì bēi júzishuǐ.** *(joo-zuh-shway)*
(M)   orange juice

Tāmen _____ **yì bēi píjiǔ.** *(pee-jee-oo)*
(M)   beer

(ssee-oo-yow)
xūyào
to need

Wǒ _____ **yì jiān fángjiān.** *(yee) (jee-ahn)(fahng-jee-ahn)*
one (M)   room

Nǐ _xūyào/_____ **yì jiān fángjiān.** *(yee) (jee-ahn)(fahng-jee-ahn)*

Tā _____ **yì jiān fángjiān.**

Wǒmen _____ **yì jiān fángjiān.**

Tāmen _____ **yì jiān fángjiān.**

❏	**hǎitān** *(hi-tahn)*	....	beach	_____
❏	**hǎiwài** *(hi-why)*	....	overseas	_____
❏	**hǎiwān** *(hi-wahn)*	....	bay, gulf	_____
❏	**hǎiwèi** *(hi-way)*	....	seafood	_____
❏	**hǎiyáng** *(hi-yahng)*	....	ocean	_____

海
hǎi

Now take a break, walk around the room, take a deep breath and do the next **liù ge dòngcí.**
(lee-oo) *(dwong-tsih)*
six verbs

(jee-ow)
jiào
to be called/named

> Wǒ jiào Mǎlì.

Wǒ __jiào/_____ Yuēhàn. *(yoo-eh-hahn)*

Nǐ _____ Mǎlì. *(mah-lee)*

Tā _____ Jiàn. *(jee-ahn)*

Wǒmen _____ Yuēhàn, Mǎlì hé Jiàn. *(huh)* and

Tāmen _____ Yuēhàn, Mǎlì hé Jiàn.

(my)
mǎi
to buy

Wǒ _____ yí liàng zìxíngchē. *(yee)* *(zih-sseeng-chuh)*
one (M) bicycle

Nǐ _____ yí pán sèlā. *(suh-lah)*
(M) salad

Tā _____ yì zhāng huàr. *(jahng)* *(hwahr)*
(M) picture

Wǒmen _____ yí ge zhōng. *(jwong)*
(M) clock

Tāmen _____ yí ge táidēng. *(tah-muhn)* *(tie-dung)*
table **lamp**

(shwoh)
shuō
to speak

> Nín zhǎo!

Wǒ _____ Zhōngwén.

Nǐ __shuō/_____ Fǎwén. *(fah-wuhn)*
French

Tā _____ Yīngwén. *(yeeng-wuhn)*
English

Wǒmen _____ Rìwén. *(ree-wuhn)*
Japanese

Nǐmen _____ Déwén. *(nee-muhn)* *(duh-wuhn)*
German

(joo)
zhù
to live/reside

Wǒ _____ zài Zhōngguó. *(zi)*
in

Nǐ _____ zài Fǎguó. *(fah-gwoh)*
France

Tā _____ zài Měiguó. *(may-gwoh)*

Wǒmen _____ zài Ōuzhōu. *(woh-muhn)* *(oh-joh)*
Europe

Nǐmen __zhù/_____ zài Déguó. *(duh-gwoh)*
Germany

(jee-ow)
jiào
to order

Wǒ _____ yì bēi shuǐ. *(bay)* *(shway)*
one glass water

Nǐ _____ yì bēi jiǔ. *(jee-oo)*
(M) wine

Tā __jiào/_____ yì bēi júzishuǐ. *(joo-zuh-shway)*
orange juice

Wǒmen _____ yì bēi chá.

Tāmen _____ yì bēi niúnǎi. *(nee-oo-ni)*
milk

(teeng-lee-oo)
tíngliú
to stay

Wǒ _____ wǔ tiān. *(tee-ahn)*
days

Nǐ _____ sān tiān.

Tā _____ liǎng tiān.

Wǒmen _____ liù tiān.

Tāmen _____ bā tiān.

☐ **fàn** *(fahn)*	meal	
☐ **fànguǎn** *(fahn-gwahn)*	restaurant	
☐ **wǎnfàn** *(wahn-fahn)*	supper	饭
☐ **wǔfàn** *(woo-fahn)*	lunch	*fàn*
☐ **zǎofàn** *(zow-fahn)*	breakfast	

44

Shì, *(shr)* yes, it is hard to get used to all those **xīn cí.** *(sseen) (tsih)* new Just keep practicing and before **nǐ** know it, **nǐ** will be using them naturally. **Xiànzài** *(ssee-ahn-zi)* is a perfect time to turn to the back of this **shū,** clip out your verb flash cards and start flashing. Don't skip over your free **cí** either. Check them off in the box provided as **nǐ xuéxí** *(ssee-yoo-eh-ssee)* learn each one. See if **nǐ** can fill in the blanks below. The answers **zài** *(zi)* are at the bottom of **zhèi yè.** *(juh-ay) (yeh)* this

1. _____

                                      (I speak Chinese.)

2. _____

                                      (We learn Chinese.)

3. _____

                                      (She needs ten yuan.)

4. _____

                                      (He comes from Canada.)

5. _____

                                      (They live in China.)

6. _____

                                      (You buy a book.)

In the following Steps, **nǐ** will be introduced to more verbs and **nǐ** should drill them in exactly the same way as **nǐ** did in this section. Look up the **xīn cí** *(sseen) (tsih)* new in your **cídiǎn** *(tsih-dee-ahn)* dictionary and make up your own sentences. Try out your **xīn cí** *(sseen)* for that's how you make them yours to use on your holiday. Remember, the more **nǐ** practice **xiànzài,** the more enjoyable your trip will be. **Zhù nǐ shùnlì!** *(joo)* wish *(nee)* *(shoon-lee)* good luck

(jee) (dee-ahn) (luh)
Jǐ diǎn le?
what time is it

Nǐ know **zěnme** *(zuhn-muh)* to tell the **tiān** *(tee-ahn)* of the **xīngqī** *(sseeng-chee)* and the **yuè** *(yoo-eh)* of the **nián,** *(nee-ahn)* so **xiànzài** let's learn
how / days / week / months / year

to tell time. Punctuality **zài** *(zi)* **Zhōngguó** is **hěn** *(huhn)* **zhòngyào,** *(jwong-yow)* not to mention the need to catch
in / important

huǒchē *(hwoh-chuh)* and arrive on time. **Zhěr** *(juhr)* **shì** *(shr)* the "basics." Notice that **le** *(luh)* is often used to complete
trains / here / are

sentences in **Zhōngwén.**

What time is it?	=	*(jee) (dee-ahn) (luh)* **Jǐ diǎn le?** _____
time	=	*(shr-jee-ahn)* **shíjiān** _____
o'clock	=	*(dee-ahn)* **diǎn** _____
minute	=	*(fuhn)* **fēn** _____
a quarter (15 minutes)	=	*(shr-woo) (fuhn)* **shíwǔ fēn** _____
hour	=	*(ssee-ow-shr)* **xiǎoshí** _____
half past	=	*(bahn)* **bàn** _____
noon	=	*(jwong-woo)* **zhōngwǔ** _____
midnight	=	*(woo-yeh)* **wǔyè** _____

Xiànzài quiz yourself. Fill in the missing letters below.

midnight = | w | | y | | half past = | b | | | minute = | f | |

a quarter = | s | h | | ǔ | × | f | | n |

time = | | | í | j | i | | o'clock = | d | i | |

and finally   when = | s | | | | e | × | s | | | | | u |

☐ **fáng** *(fahng)*	....	room, apartment	_____
☐ **fángdōng** *(fahng-dwong)*	....	landlord	房 _____
☐ **fángkè** *(fahng-kuh)*	....	tenant	_____
☐ **fángzi** *(fahng-zuh)*	....	house	*fǎng* _____
☐ **shuìfáng** *(shway-fahng)*	....	bedroom	

Xiànzài, zěnme *(zuhn-muh)* are these **cí** *(tsih)* used? Study the examples below. When **nǐ** think it through, it really is not too difficult. Don't forget that **liǎng** *(lee-ahng)* means "two" in **Zhōngwén** as does **èr** *(ur)*.

Wǔ diǎn. *(woo) (dee-ahn)*
five   o'clock

| 5:00 |

Wǔ diǎn. Wǔ diǎn. Wǔ diǎn.

Wǔ diǎn shí fēn. *(shr) (fuhn)*
ten   minutes

| 5:10 |

_____

Wǔ diǎn shíwǔ fēn. *(shr-woo)*

| 5:15 |

_____

Wǔ diǎn èrshí fēn. *(ur-shr)*

| 5:20 |

_____

Wǔ diǎn bàn. *(bahn)*
(+) half

| 5:30 |

_____

Wǔ diǎn sìshí fēn. *(sih-shr)*

| 5:40 |

_____

Wǔ diǎn sìshíwǔ fēn. *(sih-shr-woo)*

| 5:45 |

_____

Wǔ diǎn wǔshí fēn. *(woo-shr)*

| 5:50 |

_____

Liù diǎn. *(lee-oo)*
o'clock

| 6:00 |

_____

See how **zhòngyào** *(jwong-yow)* it is to learn the **shùzì**? Answer the following **wèntí** *(wuhn-tee)* based on the **zhōng** *(jwong)*
important   numbers   questions   clocks
below. **Jǐ diǎn le?** *(jee) (luh)*

1. | 8:00 | _____

2. | 7:15 | _____

3. | 4:30 | _____

4. | 9:20 | _____

When **nǐ** answer a **shíjiān** *(shr-jee-ahn)* **wèntí,** *(wuhn-tee)* it is not necessary to say **"fēn"** *(fuhn)* after the number of minutes

time · question

if the number is larger than ten.

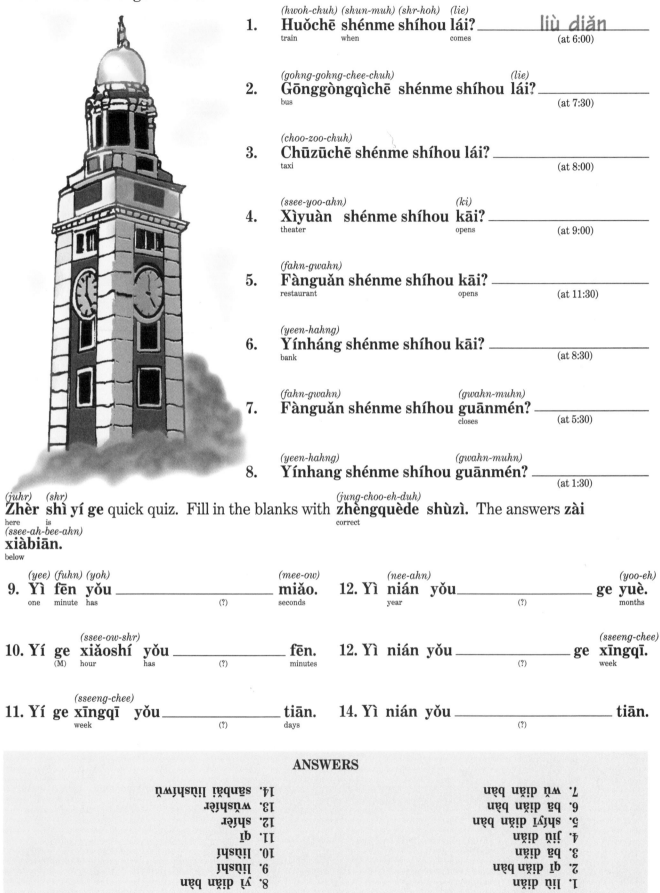

1. **Huǒchē** *(hwoh-chuh)* **shénme** *(shun-muh)* **shíhou** *(shr-hoh)* **lái?** *(lie)* ___liù diǎn___
   train · when · comes · (at 6:00)

2. **Gōnggòngqìchē** *(gohng-gohng-chee-chuh)* **shénme shíhou lái?** *(lie)* _____
   bus · (at 7:30)

3. **Chūzūchē** *(choo-zoo-chuh)* **shénme shíhou lái?** _____
   taxi · (at 8:00)

4. **Xìyuàn** *(ssee-yoo-ahn)* **shénme shíhou kāi?** *(ki)* _____
   theater · opens · (at 9:00)

5. **Fànguǎn** *(fahn-gwahn)* **shénme shíhou kāi?** _____
   restaurant · opens · (at 11:30)

6. **Yínháng** *(yeen-hahng)* **shénme shíhou kāi?** _____
   bank · (at 8:30)

7. **Fànguǎn** *(fahn-gwahn)* **shénme shíhou guānmén?** *(gwahn-muhn)* _____
   closes · (at 5:30)

8. **Yínhang** *(yeen-hahng)* **shénme shíhou guānmén?** *(gwahn-muhn)* _____
   (at 1:30)

Zhèr *(juhr)* **shì** *(shr)* **yí ge** quick quiz. Fill in the blanks with **zhěngquède** *(jung-choo-eh-duh)* **shùzì.** The answers **zài**

here · is · correct

xiàbiān. *(ssee-ah-bee-ahn)*

below

9. **Yì fēn** *(yee)(fuhn)(yoh)* **yǒu** _____ **miǎo.** *(mee-ow)*
   one · minute · has · (?) · seconds

12. **Yì nián** *(nee-ahn)* **yǒu** _____ **ge yuè.** *(yoo-eh)*
   year · (?) · months

10. **Yí ge xiǎoshí** *(ssee-ow-shr)* **yǒu** _____ **fēn.**
   (M) · hour · has · (?) · minutes

12. **Yì nián yǒu** _____ **ge xīngqī.** *(sseeng-chee)*
   (?) · week

11. **Yí ge xīngqī** *(sseeng-chee)* **yǒu** _____ **tiān.**
   week · (?) · days

14. **Yì nián yǒu** _____ **tiān.**
   (?)

Do **nǐ** remember your greetings from earlier? It is a good time to review them as they will
always be **hěn** *(huhn)* **zhòngyào.** *(jwong-yow)*
very   important

(shahng-woo)   *(ruhn-muhn)* *(shwoh)*   *(neen)* *(zow)*
Shàngwǔ bā diǎn rénmen shuō, "Nín zǎo!"
morning   eight   people   say   good morning

(shwoh) *(shun-muh)*
Rénmen shuō shénme? _____ Nín zǎo! Nín zǎo! Nín zǎo!
what

(ssee-ah-woo)   *(shwoh)* *(nee)* *(how)*
Xiàwǔ yì diǎn rénmen shuō, "Nǐ hǎo ma?"
afternoon   how are you

(ruhn-muhn)
Rénmen shuō shénme? _____

(ssee-ah-woo)   *(chahng-chahng)*   *(meeng-tee-ahn)* *(jee-ahn)*
Xiàwǔ sān diǎn rénmen chángcháng shuō, "Míngtiān jiàn."
afternoon   often   see you tomorrow

(ruhn-muhn)
Rénmen shuō shénme? _____

(wahng-shahng)   *(shr)*   *(wahn)* *(ahn)*
Wǎnshàng shí diǎn rénmen shuō, "Wǎn ān!"
evening   good night

(ruhn-muhn)
Rénmen shuō shénme? _____

Remember the meaning of **Zhōngwén cí** varies depending upon the tone used. Look at the two
words **mǎi** *(my)* and **mài** *(my)*. Notice the differences in the meanings below and then practice using the
to buy   to sell
tones by saying each **cí** out loud. Review the many words **nǐ** have learned and make a list similar
to the one below of those which are pronounced the same except for the tone.

		(bah)		*(tee)*		*(mah)*	
Tone 1:	——	**bā** = scar		**tī** = ladder		**mā** = mother	
Tone 2:	/	**bá** = to pull up		**tí** = to lift		**má** = hemp	
Tone 3:	∨	**bǎ** = measure word		**tǐ** = body		**mǎ** = horse	
Tone 4:	\	**bà** = father		**tì** = tears		**mà** = curse	

Don't worry. First learn your vocabulary and then play with the tones. Soon you will feel
comfortable with the different pronunciations, although it seems a bit overwhelming at first.

- ☐ **zhǐ** *(jihr)* .... paper _____
- ☐ **zhǐbì** *(jihr-bee)* .... paper currency _____
- ☐ **bàozhǐ** *(bao-jihr)* .... newspaper 纸 _____
- ☐ **wèishēngzhǐ** *(way-shuhng-jihr)* ... toilet paper *zhǐ* _____
- ☐ **zìzhǐlǒu** *(zuh-jihr-loh)* .... wastepaper basket _____

Zhèr shì liǎng ge xīn dòngcí for Step 13.
(lee-ahng) (sseen) (dwong-tsih)
two (M) new verbs

(chr)
chī _____
to eat

(huh)
hē _____
to drink

(chr)
chī
to eat

(huh)
hē
to drink

Wǒ _____	*(shway-gwoh)* **shuǐguǒ.** fresh fruit
Nǐ _____	*(zow-fahn)* **zǎofàn.** breakfast
Tā _____	*(yoo-we)* **yú.** fish
Wǒmen _____	*(roh)* **ròu.** meat
(nee-muhn) Nǐmen _____	*(jee-dahn)* **jīdàn.** eggs
Tāmen _____	*(joo-roh)* **zhūròu.** pork

Wǒ _____	*(nee-oo-ni)* **niúnǎi.** milk
Nǐ _hē/_____	*(joo-zuh-shway)* **júzishuǐ.** orange juice
Tā _____	**jiǔ.** wine
(woh-muhn) Wǒmen _____	**chá.**
Nǐmen _____	**kāfēi.**
Tāmen _____	*(kwahng-choo-ahn) (shway)* **kuàngquán shuǐ.** mineral water

(tsih)
Remember that **"c"** as in **"cí"** is pronounced like the "ts" in "its." Practice this sound with the

following words:
(tsuh-swoh) **cèsuǒ,** lavatory
(tswong) **cóng,** from
(tsahn-jeen) **cānjīn,** napkin
(tsow) **cǎo,** grass
(tsi) **cài,** vegetables
(tsi-dahn) **càidān,** menu
(tsahn-chuh) **cānchē.** dining car

❐ **huǒ** *(hwoh)*	fire, flame		_____
❐ **huǒchái** *(hwoh-chi)*	match		_____
❐ **huǒchē** *(hwoh-chuh)*	train	火	_____
❐ **huǒshān** *(hwoh-shahn)*	volcano		_____
❐ **huǒjiàn** *(hwoh-jee-ahn)*	rocket	*huǒ*	_____

Nǐ have learned a lot of material in the last few steps and that means it is time to quiz yourself. Don't panic, this is just for you and no one else needs to know how **nǐ** did. Remember, this is a chance to review, find out what **nǐ** remember and what **nǐ** need to spend more time on. After **nǐ** have finished, check your answers in the glossary at the back of this book. Circle the correct answers.

kāfēi	tea	coffee
bù	yes	no
gūgu	aunt	uncle
yánsè	house	color
xuéxí	to drink	to learn
yèlǐ	morning	night
xīngqīwǔ	Friday	Tuesday
shuō	to live	to speak
xiàtiān	summer	winter
qián	money	page
shí	nine	ten
miànbāo	spoon	bread

jiātíng	seven	family
xiǎohái	children	grandfather
niúnǎi	butter	(milk)
yán	pepper	salt
shàngbiān	under	over
yīshēng	man	doctor
qīyuè	June	July
zōngjiào	kitchen	religion
wǒ yǒu	I would like	I have
mǎi	to order	to buy
míngtiān	yesterday	tomorrow
huáng	good	yellow

(nee) (how) (mah)
Nǐ hǎo ma? <u>What time is it?</u> <u>How are you?</u> Well, how are you after this quiz?

❏ **huā/huār** *(hwah/hwahr)*	flower	
❏ **huā duǒ** *(hwah)(dwoh)*	blossom	花
❏ **huā píng** *(hwah)(peeng)*	flower vase	
❏ **huā quān** *(hwah)(chwahn)*	wreath	*huā*
❏ **huā shù** *(hwah)(shoo)*	bouquet	

14   (dwong) (ssee) (bay) (nahn)
Dōng - Xī, Běi - Nán
east   west   north   south

While in **Zhōngguó,** **nǐ** *(nee)* *you* will no doubt use a **dìtú.** *(dee-too)* *map* Study the direction words **xiàbiān** *(ssee-ah-bee-ahn)* *below* until **nǐ** are familiar with them and can recognize them on a **dìtú.** *(dee-too)* *map*

| **dōng** *(dwong)* east | **xī** *(ssee)* west | **běi** *(bay)* north | **nán** *(nahn)* south |

Be prepared – because on your **dìtú** *(dee-too)* *map* and when you are given directions in **Zhōngguó,** your directions will be given as "**dōngnán**" *(east-south)* and "**xīběi,**" *(west-north)* rather than "southeast" and "northwest." Also notice how the direction words are combined with the word **biān** *(bee-ahn)* *side* and **fāng** *(fahng)* *direction* below.

běibiān *(bay-bee-ahn)* = North _____

nánbiān *(nahn-bee-ahn)* = South _____

dōngbiān *(dwong-bee-ahn)* = East _____

xībiān *(ssee-bee-ahn)* = West _____

běifāng *(bay-fahng)* = northern _____

nánfāng *(nahn-fahng)* = southern *nánfāng*

dōngfāng *(dwong-fahng)* = eastern _____

xīfāng *(ssee-fahng)* = western _____

běi *(bay)* north _____

xī *(ssee)* west _____

dōng *(dwong)* east _____

nán *(nahn)* south _____

zuǒ *(zwoh)*

yìzhí zǒu *(yee-jihr) (zoh)*

yòu *(yoh)*

_____ (left)

_____ (straight ahead)

_____ (right)

☐ **cháhuā** *(chah-hwah)*	camelia		_____
☐ **júhuā** *(joo-hwah)*	chrysanthemum	花	_____
☐ **lánhuā** *(lahn-hwah)*	orchid		_____
☐ **méiguìhuā** *(may-gway-hwah)*	rose	*huā*	_____
☐ **xuěhuā** *(ssee-oo-eh-hwah)*	snowflake		_____

These **cí** can go a long way. Say them aloud each time you write them in the blanks below.

(cheeng)
qǐng _____
please

(ssee-eh-ssee-eh)
xièxie _____
thank you

(dway-boo-chee) (cheeng-wuhn)
duìbùqǐ / qǐngwèn _____
excuse me　　　　excuse me, may I ask

(boo) (ssee-eh)
bú xiè _____
you're welcome

(juhr) *(shr)* *(huhn)* *(dee-ahn-sseeng-duh)* *(dway-hwah)*
Zhèr shì liǎng ge hěn diǎnxíngde duìhuà for someone who is trying to find something.
　　　　　 two　　　 very　 typical　　　　 conversations

Write them out in the blanks below.

Zhāng Sān:　　*(cheeng-wuhn)*　　　　　　　　*(loo-we-gwahn)* *(zi)*
　　　　　　　Qǐngwèn, Běijīng Lǚguǎn zài nǎr?
　　　　　　　excuse me, may I ask　　　　　　　　　is

　　　　　　　_____

Lǐ Sì:　　*(yee-jihr)* *(zoh)* *(zi)* *(zwoh-bee-ahn)*
　　　　　Yìzhí zǒu zài zuǒbiān.
　　　　　　　　　　　 on　　 left-hand side

　　　　　_____

　　　　　Nà shì Běijīng Lǚguǎn.
　　　　　　　　　　　　　　 (loo-we-gwahn)

　　　　　_____

Zhāng Sān:　　　　　　　　　　　　*(bwoh-woo-gwahn)*
　　　　　　　Qǐngwèn, Zhōngguó Bówùguǎn zài nǎr?
　　　　　　　may I ask　　　　　　　 museum

　　　　　　　_____

Lǐ Sì:　　　　 *(juhr)* *(yoh)* *(jwahn)* *(yee-jihr)* *(zoh)*
　　　　　Zài zhèr yòu zhuǎn, yìzhí zǒu,
　　　　　from　 here　 right　 turn　　 straight　 ahead

　　　　　_____

　　　　　　　　　(bwoh-woo-gwahn) *(yoh-bee-ahn)*
　　　　　Zhōngguó Bówùguǎn zài yòubiān.
　　　　　　　　　　　　　　　　　　 right side

　　　　　_____

❑ **zì** *(zih)*	Chinese character	
❑ **zìdiǎn** *(zih-dee-ahn)*	character dictionary	字
❑ **zìtiáo** *(zih-tee-ow)*	note	
❑ **zìmǔ** *(zih-moo)*	letters of alphabet	
❑ **zìmù** *(zih-moo)*	subtitles	*zì*

Are **nǐ** lost? There is no need to be lost if **nǐ xuéxí** *(ssee-yoo-eh-ssee)* le the basic direction **cí**. Do not try to memorize these **duìhuà** *(dway-hwah)* conversations because **nǐ** will never be looking for precisely these places. One day, **nǐ** might need to ask for directions to "**Tàiyáng** *(tie-yahng)* sun **Fànguǎn**" restaurant or "**Lìshǐ** *(lee-shr)* history **Bówùguǎn**." *(bwoh-woo-gwahn)* Learn the key direction **cí** and be sure **nǐ** can find your destination. **Nǐ** may want to buy a guidebook to start planning which places **nǐ** would like to visit. Practice asking directions to these special places. What if the person responding to your **wèntí** *(wuhn-tee)* question answers too quickly for **nǐ** to understand the entire reply? Practice saying,

(dway-boo-chee)		*(boo)*	*(dwong)*	*(cheeng)*	*(zi)*	*(shwoh)*	*(yee-bee-ahn)*	*(ssee-eh-ssee-eh)*
Duìbùqǐ.	**Wǒ**	**bù**	**dǒng.**	**Qǐng**	**zài**	**shuō**	**yíbiàn.**	**Xièxie.**
excuse me		not	understand	please	again	say	once	

Xiànzài, say it again and then write it out below.

_____
(Excuse me. I do not understand. Please repeat. Thank you.)

Shì, yes it is difficult at first but don't give up! **Shénme shíhou** *(shr-hoh)* when the directions are repeated, **nǐ** will be able to understand if **nǐ** have learned the key **cí**. Let's review by writing them in the blanks below.

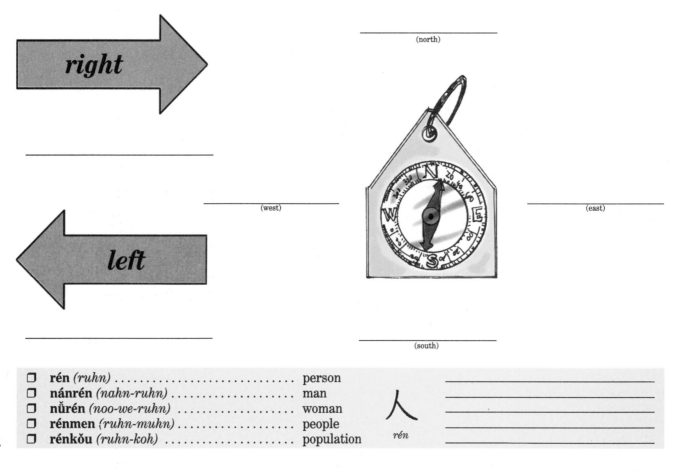

right

left

_____ (north)

_____ (west)

_____ (east)

_____ (south)

☐ **rén** *(ruhn)* . . . . person   _____
☐ **nánrén** *(nahn-ruhn)* . . . . man   _____
☐ **nǚrén** *(noo-we-ruhn)* . . . . woman   _____
☐ **rénmen** *(ruhn-muhn)* . . . . people   _____
☐ **rénkǒu** *(ruhn-koh)* . . . . population   _____

人
rén

(juhr) *(sseen)* *(dwong-tsih)*
Zhèr shì jǐ ge xīn dòngcí.
some (M) new verbs

(shwoh)
shuō _____
to say

(dwong)
dǒng _____
to understand

(my)
mài mài, mài, mài, mài, mài
to sell

(zi) *(shwoh)* *(yee-bee-ahn)*
zài shuō yíbiàn _____
to repeat, say once again

Did you notice that the only difference between the *(dwong-tsih)* **dòngcí** *(my)* **"mài"** *(huh)* **hé** *(my)* **"mǎi"** is the tone?
verbs   to sell   and   to buy

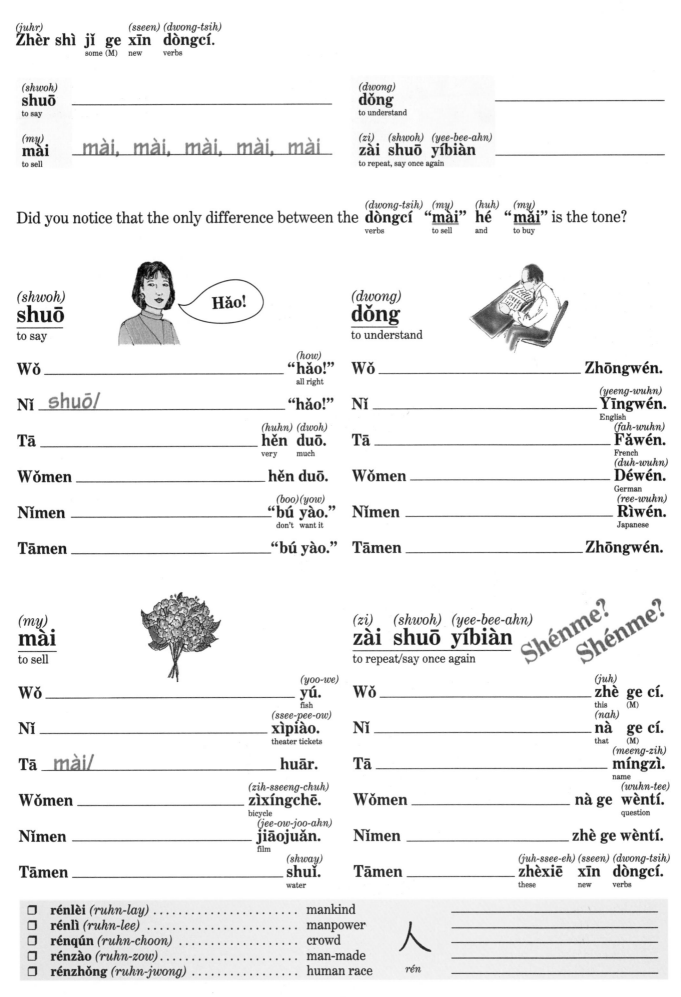

(shwoh)
shuō
to say

Wǒ _____ "**hǎo!**" *(how)* all right

Nǐ __shuō/_____ "**hǎo!**"

Tā _____ **hěn duō.** *(huhn) (dwoh)* very much

Wǒmen _____ **hěn duō.**

Nǐmen _____ "**bú yào.**" *(boo)(yow)* don't want it

Tāmen _____ "**bú yào.**"

(dwong)
dǒng
to understand

Wǒ _____ **Zhōngwén.**

Nǐ _____ **Yīngwén.** *(yeeng-wuhn)* English

Tā _____ **Fǎwén.** *(fah-wuhn)* French

Wǒmen _____ **Déwén.** *(duh-wuhn)* German

Nǐmen _____ **Rìwén.** *(ree-wuhn)* Japanese

Tāmen _____ **Zhōngwén.**

(my)
mài
to sell

Wǒ _____ **yú.** *(yoo-we)* fish

Nǐ _____ **xìpiào.** *(ssee-pee-ow)* theater tickets

Tā __mài/_____ **huār.**

Wǒmen _____ **zìxíngchē.** *(zih-sseeng-chuh)* bicycle

Nǐmen _____ **jiāojuǎn.** *(jee-ow-joo-ahn)* film

Tāmen _____ **shuǐ.** *(shway)* water

(zi) *(shwoh)* *(yee-bee-ahn)*
zài shuō yíbiàn Shénme? Shénme?
to repeat/say once again

Wǒ _____ **zhè ge cí.** *(juh)* this (M)

Nǐ _____ **nà ge cí.** *(nah)* that (M)

Tā _____ **míngzì.** *(meeng-zih)* name

Wǒmen _____ **nà ge wèntí.** *(wuhn-tee)* question

Nǐmen _____ **zhè ge wèntí.**

Tāmen _____ **zhèxiē xīn dòngcí.** *(juh-ssee-eh) (sseen) (dwong-tsih)* these new verbs

❏ **rénlèi** *(ruhn-lay)*	mankind	_____
❏ **rénlì** *(ruhn-lee)*	manpower	_____
❏ **rénqún** *(ruhn-choon)*	crowd	_____
❏ **rénzào** *(ruhn-zow)*	man-made	_____
❏ **rénzhǒng** *(ruhn-jwong)*	human race	_____

人
rén

15

(shahng-bee-ahn) *(ssee-ah-bee-ahn)*

Shàngbiān - Xiàbiān

above/over   below/under

(dwoh)(ssee-yoo-eh-ssee) (jee)   *(juhr) (yoh)*   *(fahng-zuh) (chee-oo)*
Xiànzài wǒmen duō xuéxí   jǐ   ge cí. Zài Zhōngguó, zhèr yǒu yí ge fángzi. Qù your
                    more learn   several   here there is   house   go to
(shway-fahng)   *(fahng-jee-ahn)*   *(dwong-ssee)*
shuìfáng and look around the **fángjiān**. Let's **xuéxí** the **míngzì** of the **dōngxi** in the **shuìfáng**,
bedroom   room   learn   names   things

just like **wǒmen** learned the various parts of the **fángzi**.
                                                    (fahng-zih)

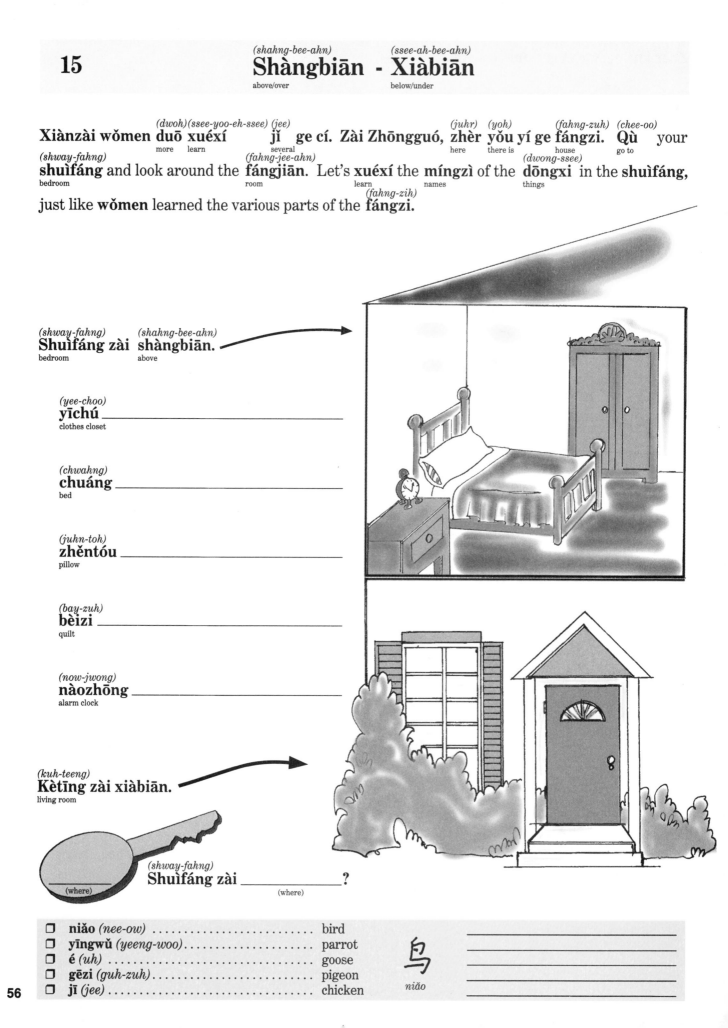

(shway-fahng)   *(shahng-bee-ahn)*
Shuìfáng zài shàngbiān.
bedroom   above

(yee-choo)
yīchú _____
clothes closet

(chwahng)
chuáng _____
bed

(juhn-toh)
zhěntóu _____
pillow

(bay-zuh)
bèizi _____
quilt

(now-jwong)
nàozhōng _____
alarm clock

(kuh-teeng)
Kètīng zài xiàbiān.
living room

(shway-fahng)
Shuìfáng zài _____?
                    (where)

(where)

❏ **niǎo** *(nee-ow)*	. . . .	bird
❏ **yīngwǔ** *(yeeng-woo)*	. . . .	parrot
❏ **é** *(uh)*	. . . .	goose
❏ **gēzi** *(guh-zuh)*	. . . .	pigeon
❏ **jī** *(jee)*	. . . .	chicken

鸟
niǎo

_____
_____
_____
_____
_____

Xiànzài, remove the next group of stickers and label these **dōngxi** in your **shuǐfáng.** *(shway-fahng)* Let's

move into the **yùshì** *(yoo-we-shr)* and do the same thing. Remember, **yùshì** *(yoo-we-shr)* means a room to bathe in. If

nǐ are in a **fànguǎn** *(fahn-gwahn)* and want the lavatory, **nǐ** want to ask for **cèsuǒ,** *(tsuh-swoh)* *not* for the **yùshì.** *(yoo-we-shr)* In

Zhōngguó, restrooms are marked with the Chinese characters 女 and 男 .

Don't confuse them! These would be two good characters to learn!

(noo-we)
nǚ
ladies' / female

(nahn)
nán
men's / male

(yoo-we-shr)
Yùshì **zài shàngbiān.**
bathroom

(jeeng-zuh)
jìngzi _____
mirror

(ssee-lee-ahn-puhn)
xǐliǎnpén _____
washstand

(mao-jeen)
máojīn _____
towel

(mah-twong)
mǎtǒng _____
toilet

(leen-yoo-we)
línyù _____
shower

Shūfáng zài *(ssee-ah-bee-ahn)* **xiàbiān.**
study   below

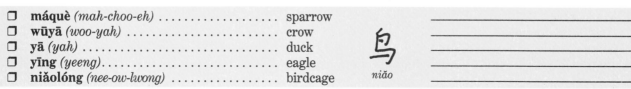

❐ **máquè** *(mah-choo-eh)*	sparrow		_____
❐ **wūyā** *(woo-yah)*	crow		_____
❐ **yā** *(yah)*	duck	鸟	_____
❐ **yīng** *(yeeng)*	eagle	*niǎo*	_____
❐ **niǎolóng** *(nee-ow-lwong)*	birdcage		_____

Do not forget to remove the next group of stickers and label these **dōngxi** *(dwong-ssee)* in your **fángzi** *(fahng-zih)*. Okay, it is time to review. Here's a quick quiz to see what you remember.

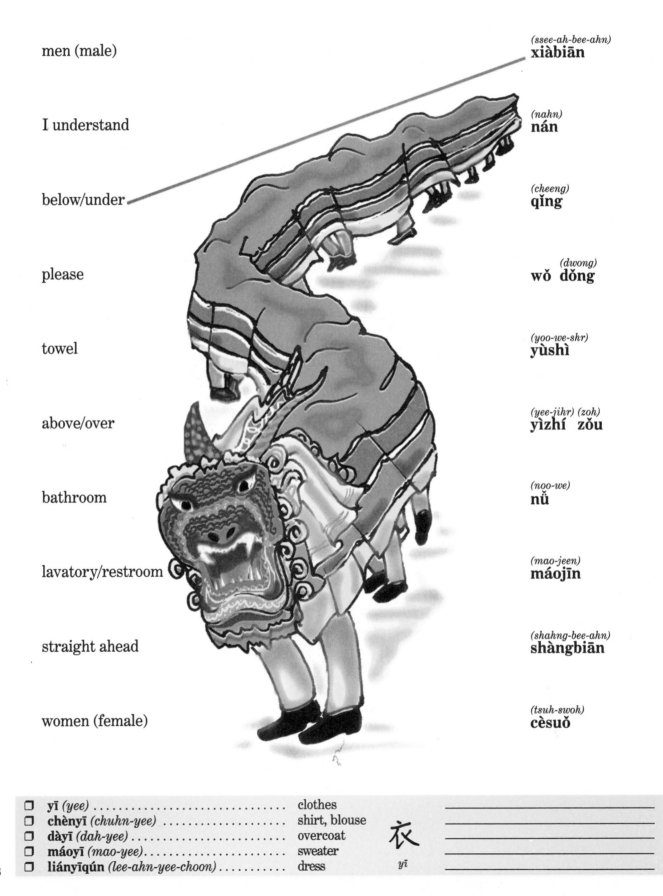

men (male)   *(ssee-ah-bee-ahn)* **xiàbiān**

I understand   *(nahn)* **nán**

below/under   *(cheeng)* **qǐng**

please   *(dwong)* **wǒ dǒng**

towel   *(yoo-we-shr)* **yùshì**

above/over   *(yee-jihr) (zoh)* **yìzhí zǒu**

bathroom   *(noo-we)* **nǚ**

lavatory/restroom   *(mao-jeen)* **máojīn**

straight ahead   *(shahng-bee-ahn)* **shàngbiān**

women (female)   *(tsuh-swoh)* **cèsuǒ**

☐ **yī** *(yee)*	clothes		_____
☐ **chènyī** *(chuhn-yee)*	shirt, blouse		_____
☐ **dàyī** *(dah-yee)*	overcoat	衣	_____
☐ **máoyī** *(mao-yee)*	sweater		_____
☐ **liányīqún** *(lee-ahn-yee-choon)*	dress	*yī*	_____

Next stop — **shūfáng**, *(shoo-fahng)* specifically **zhuōzi** *(jwoh-zuh)* or **shūzhuō** *(shoo-jwoh)* in the **shūfáng**! **Shénme** *(shun-muh)* is on the
office   table   desk   what

zhuōzi? *(jwoh-zuh)* Let's identify the **dōngxi** *(dwong-ssee)* which one normally finds in the **shūfáng** or strewn about the
                                                              things

fángzi. *(fahng-zuh)*
house

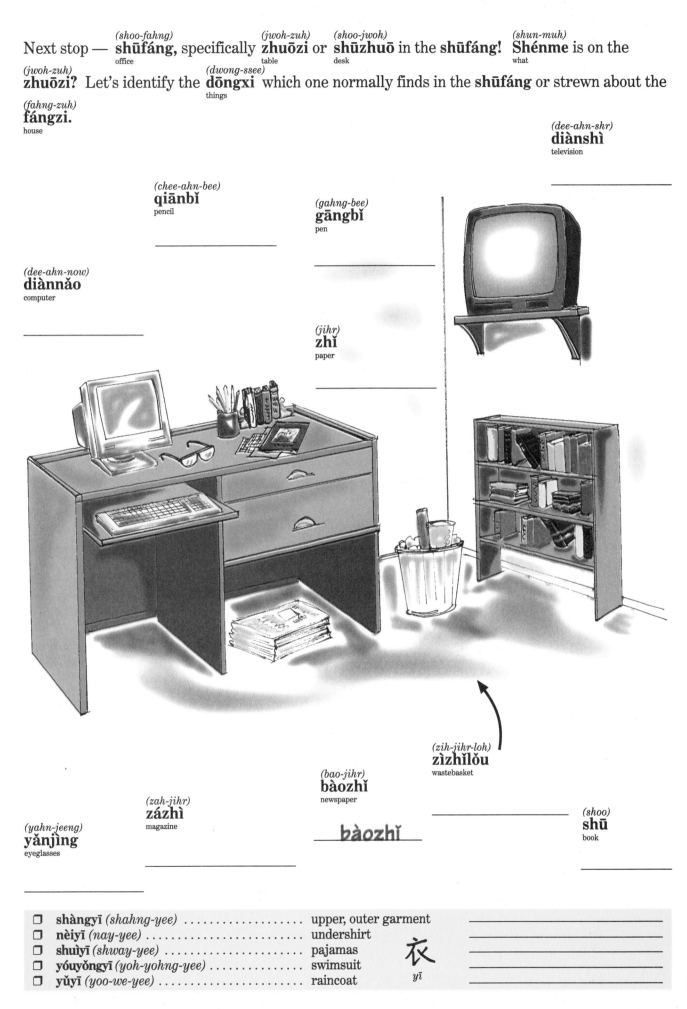

(dee-ahn-shr)
diànshì
television

(chee-ahn-bee)
qiānbǐ
pencil

(gahng-bee)
gāngbǐ
pen

(dee-ahn-now)
diànnǎo
computer

(jihr)
zhǐ
paper

(zih-jihr-loh)
zìzhǐlǒu
wastebasket

(bao-jihr)
bàozhǐ
newspaper

bàozhǐ

(zah-jihr)
zázhì
magazine

(shoo)
shū
book

(yahn-jeeng)
yǎnjìng
eyeglasses

❐ **shàngyī** *(shahng-yee)*	upper, outer garment		_____
❐ **nèiyī** *(nay-yee)*	undershirt		_____
❐ **shuìyī** *(shway-yee)*	pajamas	衣	_____
❐ **yóuyǒngyī** *(yoh-yohng-yee)*	swimsuit		_____
❐ **yǔyī** *(yoo-we-yee)*	raincoat	*yī*	_____

Don't forget these essentials!

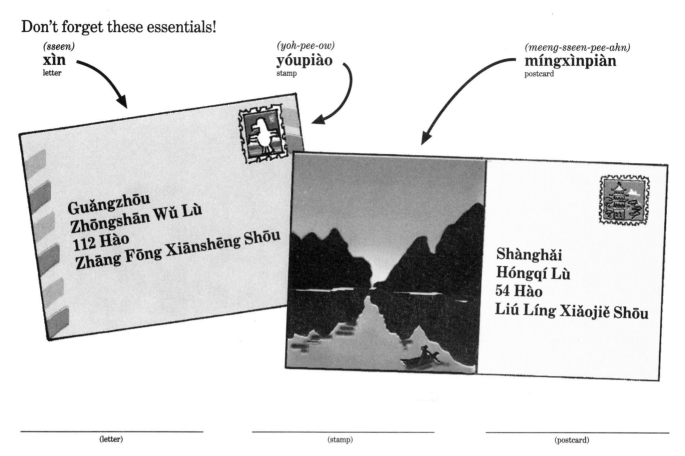

xìn *(sseen)*
letter

yóupiào *(yoh-pee-ow)*
stamp

míngxìnpiàn *(meeng-sseen-pee-ahn)*
postcard

Guǎngzhōu
Zhōngshān Wǔ Lù
112 Hào
Zhāng Fōng Xiānshēng Shōu

Shànghǎi
Hóngqí Lù
54 Hào
Liú Líng Xiǎojiě Shōu

_____   _____   _____
(letter)   (stamp)   (postcard)

Did **nǐ** notice that Chinese addresses are written in reverse order starting with the city? The

recipient's name is on the last line and is written last name, first name and title.

xiānshēng *(ssee-ahn-shuhng)* _____   **tàitài** *(tie-tie)* _____   **xiǎojiě** *(ssee-ow-jee-eh)* _____
Mr.   Mrs.   Miss

The word **"shōu"** *(shoh)* indicates the recipient and is used with both men and women. **Xiànzài** practice

saying and writing your name. **Nǐ jiào shénme míngzì? Wǒ jiào** _____.

Unless **nǐ** are very close friends, it is customary **zài Zhōngguó** to address an individual using the

appropriate title and his or her last name. In many parts of **Zhōngguó nǐ** will hear people also

addressed as **tóngzhì.** *(twong-jihr)*
comrade

Remember these key **cí.**

lù *(loo)* _____   **hào** *(how)* _____   **jiē** *(jee-eh)* _____
road   number   street

☐ **xié** *(ssee-eh)*.......................... shoes
☐ **bùxié** *(boo-ssee-eh)*.......................... cotton shoes
☐ **liángxié** *(lee-ahng-ssee-eh)*.............. sandals   鞋
☐ **qiúxié** *(chee-yoo-ssee-eh)*.............. sport shoes   *xié*
☐ **tuōxié** *(twoh-ssee-eh)*.......................... slippers

_____
_____
_____
_____
_____

60

Simple, isn't it? **Xiànzài**, after **nǐ** fill in the blanks below, go back a second time and negate all these sentences by adding **"bù"** before each verb. Don't get discouraged! Just look at how much **nǐ** have already learned and think ahead to wonderful new food, the Great Wall of China and new adventures.

(kahn-jee-ahn)
kànjiàn _____
to see

(jee)
jì _____
to send by mail, mail

(shway)
shuì _____
to sleep

(jow)
zhǎo _____
to look for

(kahn-jee-ahn)
kànjiàn
to see

Wǒ _kànjiàn/_____ *(chwahng)* **chuáng.**

Nǐ _____ *(bay-zuh)* **bèizi.**
quilt

Tā _____ *(now-jwong)* **nàozhōng.**
alarm clock

Wǒmen _____ *(ssee-lee-ahn-puhn)* **xǐliǎnpén.**

Tāmen _____ *(leen-yoo-we)* **línyù.**
shower

(jee)
jì
to mail/send by mail

Wǒ _____ *(sseen)* **xìn.**
letters

Nǐ _____ *(meeng-sseen-pee-ahn)* **míngxìnpiàn.**
postcards

Tā _____ **shū.**

Wǒmen _____ **míngxìnpiàn.**

Nǐmen _____ **xìn.**

(shway)
shuì
to sleep

Wǒ *(zi)* **zài** *(shway-fahng)* **shuìfáng** _____ .
in   bedroom

Nǐ **zài** *(fahng-zuh)* **fángzi lǐ** _____ .
inside

Tā **zài** *(kuh-teeng)* **kètīng** _____ .
living room

Wǒmen **zài** **shūfáng** _____ .

(nee-muhn) **Nǐmen zài** *(choo-fahng)* **chúfáng** _____ .
kitchen

Tāmen **zài** *(dee-see-ah-shr)* **dìxiàshì** _____ .
basement

(jow)
zhǎo
to look for

Wǒ _____ *(yoh-pee-ow)* **yóupiào.**

Nǐ _____ *(jihr)* **zhǐ.**

Tā _____ *(bao-jihr)* **bàozhǐ.**

(woh-muhn) **Wǒmen** _____ *(gahng-bee)* **gāngbǐ.**

Nǐmen _zhǎo/_____ *(zah-jihr)* **zázhì.**

Tāmen _____ *(hwahr)* **huàr.**

☐	**qín** *(cheen)*	musical instrument	_____
☐	**fēngqín** *(fung-cheen)*	organ	_____
☐	**kǒuqín** *(koh-cheen)*	harmonica	_____
☐	**gāngqín** *(gahng-cheen)*	piano	_____
☐	**tíqín** *(tee-cheen)*	violin	_____

琴
qín

61

Before **nǐ** proceed with the next step, **qǐng,** *(cheeng)* identify all the items below.

(zah-jihr)
zázhì

(zih-jihr-loh)
zìzhǐlǒu

míngxìnpiàn

shū

(yoh-pee-ow)
yóupiào

(jihr)
zhǐ

gāngbǐ

(chee-ahn-bee)
qiānbǐ

xìn

yǎnjìng

(bao-jihr)
bàozhǐ

diànshì

(dee-ahn-now)
diànnǎo

☐	**máo** *(mao)*	wool	
☐	**máobǐ** *(mao-bee)*	writing brush	
☐	**máojīn** *(mao-jeen)*	towel	毛
☐	**máopí** *(mao-pee)*	fur	
☐	**máoyī** *(mao-yee)*	sweater	*máo*

(yoh-joo-we)
Yóujú
post office

Xiànzài nǐ know how to count, how to ask **wèntí**, how to use **dòngcí** *(dwong-tsih)* with the "plug-in" formula,

how to make statements and how to describe something, be it the location of **yí ge lǚguǎn** *(loo-we-gwahn)*
hotel

huòzhě *(hwoh-juh)* **yí ge fángzide** *(fahng-zuh-duh)* **yánsè.** *(yahn-suh)* **Xiànzài** let's take the basics that **nǐ** have learned and expand
or house's color

them in special areas that will be most helpful in your travels. What does everyone do on a

holiday? Send **míngxìnpiàn,** *(meeng-sseen-pee-ahn)* of course. Let's learn exactly how **Zhōngguó yóujú** *(yoh-joo-we)* works.
postcards post office

(sseen)
xìn . . .

(dow) *(may-gwoh)*
dào Měiguó
to

(ssee-bahn-yah)
dào Xībānyá
Spain

dào Yīngguó

(yee-dah-lee)
dào Yìdàlì
Italy

Zài Zhōngguó, yóujú *(yoh-joo-we)* has everything. **Nǐ jì xìn, míngxìnpiàn** *(jee)(sseen)(meeng-sseen-pee-ahn)* and **dǎ diànbào.** *(dah)(dee-ahn-bao)* **Nǐ** also
send make telegrams

mǎi yóupiào *(yoh-pee-ow)* in the **yóujú.** *(yoh-joo-we)* **Zhōngguóde yóutǒng** *(yoh-twong)* **shì** *(shr)* **lǜsè** *(loo-we-suh)* **de.** If **nǐ xūyào** *(ssee-oo-yow)* to call home
stamps mailbox green need

dào Měiguó *(dow)* or **Yīngguó,** sometimes this can also be done at **yóujú** *(yoh-joo-we)* as well as from a private
to

home or from your hotel.

❏	**dòu** *(doh)*	bean	
❏	**dòufu** *(doh-foo)*	bean curd	
❏	**dòushā** *(doh-shah)*	bean paste	
❏	**dòuyá** *(doh-yah)*	bean sprouts	
❏	**dòuyóu** *(doh-yoh)*	soybean oil	豆 *dòu*

Zhèr shì the necessary **yóuzhèng cí.** *(yoh-jung)* *postal* Practice them aloud and write them in the blanks.

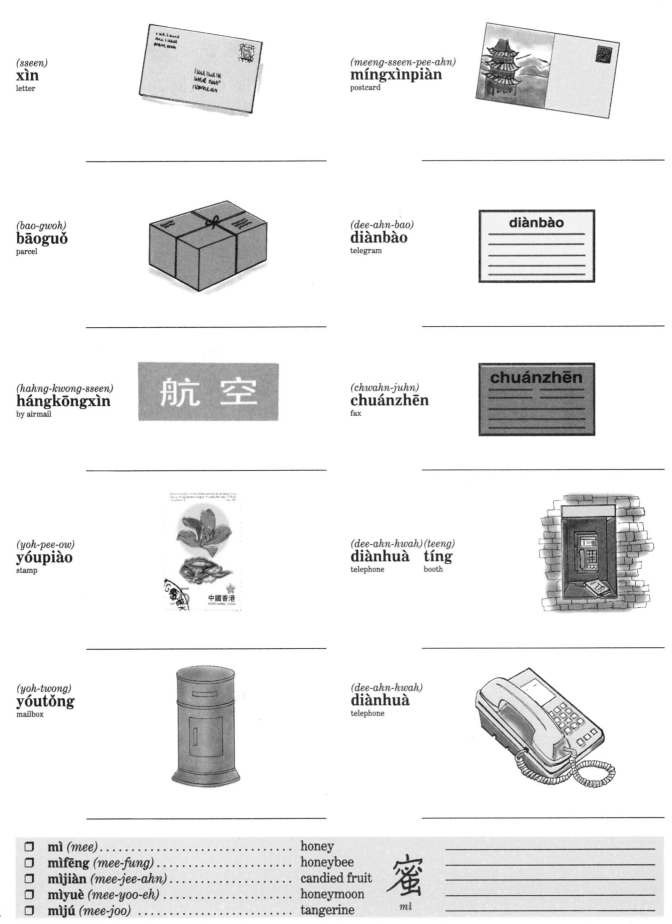

(sseen)
xìn
letter

(meeng-sseen-pee-ahn)
míngxìnpiàn
postcard

(bao-gwoh)
bāoguǒ
parcel

(dee-ahn-bao)
diànbào
telegram

diànbào

(hahng-kwong-sseen)
hángkōngxìn
by airmail

航 空

(chwahn-juhn)
chuánzhēn
fax

chuánzhēn

(yoh-pee-ow)
yóupiào
stamp

中國香港
HONG KONG, CHINA

(dee-ahn-hwah) (teeng)
diànhuà tíng
telephone booth

(yoh-twong)
yóutǒng
mailbox

(dee-ahn-hwah)
diànhuà
telephone

☐ **mì** *(mee)*	honey	
☐ **mìfēng** *(mee-fung)*	honeybee	蜜
☐ **mìjiàn** *(mee-jee-ahn)*	candied fruit	*mì*
☐ **mìyuè** *(mee-yoo-eh)*	honeymoon	
☐ **mìjú** *(mee-joo)*	tangerine	

Next step — **nǐ** ask **wèntí** like those **xiàbiānde** *(ssee-ah-bee-ahn-duh)* depending on what **nǐ** would like. Repeat

below

these sentences aloud many times.

(woh) (zi) (nahr) (my) (yoh-pee-ow)
Wǒ zài nǎr mǎi yóupiào? _____
I   where buy   stamps

(meeng-sseen-pee-ahn)
Wǒ zài nǎr mǎi míngxìnpiàn? _____
postcards

(yoh) (yoh-twong)
Nǎr yǒu yóutǒng? _____
is   mailbox

(gohng-yohng) (dee-ahn-hwah)
Nǎr yǒu gōngyòng diànhuà? _____
public   telephone

(dah) (dee-ahn-hwah)
Wǒ zài nǎr dǎ diànhuà? _____
make telephone calls

(dah) (buhn-dee) (dee-ahn-hwah)
Wǒ zài nǎr dǎ běndì diànhuà? _____
make local   telephone call

(dah) (chahng-too) (dee-ahn-hwah)
Wǒ zài nǎr dǎ chángtú diànhuà? _____
make long-distance

(dwoh-shao) (chee-ahn)
Duōshao qián? _____ *Duōshao qián? Duōshao qián? Duōshao qián?*

Xiànzài, quiz yourself. See if **nǐ** can translate the following thoughts into **Zhōngwén.**

1. Where is a telephone booth? _____

2. Where do I make a telephone call? _____

3. Where do I make a local telephone call? _____

4. Where is the post office? _____

5. Where do I buy stamps? _____

6. How much is it? _____

7. Where do I send a package? _____

8. Where do I send a fax? _____

ANSWERS

8. Wǒ zài nǎr jì chuánzhēn?
7. Wǒ zài nǎr jì bāoguǒ?
6. Duōshao qián?
5. Wǒ zài nǎr mǎi yóupiào?

4. Yóujú zài nǎr?
3. Wǒ zài nǎr dǎ běndì diànhuà?
2. Wǒ zài nǎr dǎ diànhuà?
1. Diànhuà tíng zài nǎr?

Zhèr shì jǐ ge dòngcí.
(shr) *(jee)*
are several

(dah)
dǎ _____
to make (telephone call, telegram, etc.)

(ssee-eh)
xiě _____
to write

(gay)
gěi _____
to give

(foo) (chee-ahn)
fù qián _____
to pay

Practice these verbs by not only filling in the blanks, but by saying them aloud many, many times until **nǐ** are comfortable with the sounds and the **cí.**

(dah)
dǎ
to make

Wǒ _____ yí ge diànhuà.
one *(dee-ahn-hwah)* telephone call

Nǐ _dǎ/_____ yí ge diànbào.
(dee-ahn-bao) telegram

Tā bù _____ diànhuà.
not telephone calls

Wǒmen _____ hěn duō diànhuà.
(huhn) (dwoh) very many

Tāmen bù _____ diànbào.

(ssee-eh)
xiě
to write

Wǒ _____ yì fēng xìn.
(fung) (sseen) (M) letter

Nǐ _xiě/_____ wǔ ge cí.

Tā _____ hěn duō cí.
(huhn) (dwoh) very many

Wǒmen _____ shénme?
(shun-muh) what

Nǐmen _____ shénme?

(gay)
gěi
to give

Wǒ _____ tā yì běn shū.
(tah) (buhn) him (M)

Nǐ _gěi/_____ wǒ sì zhāng míngxìnpiàn.
(sih) (jahng) me (M)

Tā _____ tāmen hěn duō qián.
them very much money

Wǒmen _____ tā bā zhāng yóupiào.
her eight (M) *(jahng) (yoh-pee-ow)* stamps

Tāmen _____ nǐ shénme?
you what *(shun-muh)*

(foo) (chee-ahn)
fù qián
to pay

Wǒ _____ yì běn shūde _____ .
(buhn) (shoo-duh) (M) book's

Nǐ _fù/_____ qiānbǐde _qián/_ .
(chee-ahn-bee-duh) pencil's

Tā _____ gāngbǐde _____ .
(gahng-bee-duh) fountain pen's

Wǒmen _____ wǔ zhāng yóupiàode _____ .
(yoh-pee-ow-duh) stamp's

Tāmen bù _____ shénme _____ ?
what

☐ **niú** *(nee-oo)* . . . . cow
☐ **niúdú** *(nee-oo-doo)* . . . . calf
☐ **niújiǎo** *(nee-oo-jee-ow)* . . . . horn
☐ **niúzǎikù** *(nee-oo-zi-koo)* . . . . jeans
☐ **niúnǎi** *(nee-oo-ni)* . . . . milk

牛
niú

_____
_____
_____
_____

Zhèr shì some of the most important **Zhōngguó** signs. Spend some time becoming familiar with

(tah-muhn)
tāmen. Take a piece of paper and try drawing them yourself.
them

热	冷	推	拉
Hot	Cold	Push	Pull

空	出租	出售	出纳
Vacant	For Hire, For Rent	For Sale	Cashier

售票处	客满	关闭
Ticket Office	Sold Out	Closed

禁止摄影	危险	停止
No Photos Allowed	Danger	Stop

请勿触摸

Do Not Touch

一路平安

Yí lù píng ān!

67

What follows are approximate conversions, so when you order something by liters, kilograms or grams you will have an idea of what to expect and not find yourself being handed one piece of candy when you thought you ordered an entire bag.

To Convert		Do the Math		
liters (l) to gallons,	multiply by 0.26	4 liters x 0.26	=	1.04 gallons
gallons to liters,	multiply by 3.79	10 gal. x 3.79	=	37.9 liters
kilograms (kg) to pounds,	multiply by 2.2	2 kilograms x 2.2	=	4.4 pounds
pounds to kilos,	multiply by 0.46	10 pounds x 0.46	=	4.6 kg
grams (g) to ounces,	multiply by 0.035	100 grams x 0.035	=	3.5 oz.
ounces to grams,	multiply by 28.35	10 oz. x 28.35	=	283.5 g.
meters (m) to feet,	multiply by 3.28	2 meters x 3.28	=	6.56 feet
feet to meters,	multiply by 0.3	6 feet x 0.3	=	1.8 meters

For fun, take your weight in pounds and convert it into kilograms. It sounds better that way, doesn't it? How many kilometers is it from your home to school, to work, to the post office?

The Simple Versions		
one liter	=	approximately one US quart
four liters	=	approximately one US gallon
one kilo	=	approximately 2.2 pounds
100 grams	=	approximately 3.5 ounces
500 grams	=	slightly more than one pound
one meter	=	slightly more than three feet

The distance between London and **Běijīng** is approximately 5,063 miles. How many kilometers would that be? It is 9,525 miles between New York and Singapore. How many kilometers is that?

kilometers (km.) to miles,	multiply by 0.62	1000 km. x 0.62	=	620 miles
miles to kilometers,	multiply by 1.6	1000 miles x 1.6	=	1,600 km.

Inches	1		2		3		4		5		6		7

To convert centimeters into inches, multiply by 0.39   Example: 9 cm. x 0.39 = 3.51 in.

To convert inches into centimeters, multiply by 2.54   Example: 4 in. x 2.54 = 10.16 cm.

cm 1	2	3	4	5	6	7	8	9	10	11	12	13	14	15	16	17	18

(jahng-dahn)
Zhàngdān
the bill

Zài Zhōngguó, there are also bills to pay. **Nǐ** have just finished your meal and **nǐ** would like to pay the bill. **Nǐ** **zěnme** **fù** **qián?** **Nǐ** **jiào** the **fúwùyuán.** The **fúwùyuán** will normally reel
(zuhn-muh) (foo) (chee-ahn) *(jee-ow)* *(foo-woo-yoo-ahn)*
how pay call service person

off what **nǐ** have eaten while writing rapidly. **Tā** will then **gěi** you a slip of **zhǐ,** and say,
(gay) *(jihr)*
give paper

(yee-gohng) *(woo-shr-lee-oo)* *(kwhy)* *(mao)*
" **Yígòng** **wǔshíliù** **kuài** **liù** **máo.** "
altogether

Nǐ will take your **zhàngdān** to the counter to pay the cashier **huòzhě** **nǐ** **gěi** **fúwùyuán** **qián**
(jahng-dahn) *(hwoh-juh)* *(gay)* *(chee-ahn)*
bill or give money

and **zhàngdān.**
(jahng-dahn)

Remember that, **zài Zhōngguó,** it is not customary to leave a tip. Also do not be surprised if the
(foo-woo-yoo-ahn)
fúwùyuán does not thank you – this is also not a custom **zài Zhōngguó.** Sound confusing? Not

really, just **xīn** and different. Every night after dinner practice asking for the **zhàngdān** in
(sseen) *(jahng-dahn)*

Zhōngwén.

(loo-we-gwahn)
Note: **Lǚguǎn** is a general term for hotels. Many foreign tourists visiting China stay in a
(been-gwahn) (jee-oo-dee-ahn)
bīnguǎn or **jiǔdiàn** which are more comfortably appointed.

❏ **niúpái** *(nee-oo-pie)*	beefsteak		_____
❏ **niúpí** *(nee-oo-pee)*	leather		_____
❏ **niúpí zhǐ** *(nee-oo-pee)(jihr)*	brown paper	牛	_____
❏ **niúròu** *(nee-oo-roh)*	beef		_____
❏ **niúwěi** *(nee-oo-way)*	oxtail	*niú*	_____

Remember these key **cí** when dining out **zài Zhōngguó.**

(foo-woo-yoo-ahn)
fúwùyuán _____
waiter

(shoh-joo)
shōujù _____
receipt

(jahng-dahn)
zhàngdān   zhàngdān, zhàngdān
bill

(cheeng-wuhn)
qǐngwèn _____
excuse me, may I ask . . .

(tsi-dahn)
càidān _____
menu

(boo) (ssee-eh)
bú xiè _____
you're welcome

(dway-boo-chee)
duìbùqǐ _____
excuse me

(ssee-eh-ssee-eh)
xièxie _____
thank you

(cheeng)
qǐng _____
please

(gay) (woh)
gěi wǒ _____
give me

(juhr) (shr)
Zhèr shì yí ge sample *(dway-hwah)* **duìhuà** involving paying the *(jahng-dahn)* **zhàngdān** when leaving a *(loo-we-gwahn)* **lǚguǎn.**
this   is   (M)   conversation   bill

Zhāng Sān: Xiānshēng, wǒ xiǎng *(jee-eh)* **jié zhàng.**
                                                  want   to clear

   Xiānshēng, wǒ xiǎng jié zhàng.   Xiānshēng, wǒ xiǎng jié zhàng.

(loo-we-gwahn) (jeeng-lee)
Lǚguǎn Jīnglǐ: *(cheeng-wuhn)* **Qǐngwèn nǎ ge** *(fahng-jee-ahn)* **fángjiān?**
           manager   excuse me, may I ask   which   room

_____

Zhāng Sān: **Sān bǎi** *(by)* **yì shí** *(how)* **hào.**
                        hundred   number

_____

Lǚguǎn Jīnglǐ: *(ssee-eh-ssee-eh)* **Xièxie.**   *(cheeng)* **Qǐng** *(dung)* **děng yí** *(ssee-ah)* **xià.**
                                                       please   wait   a   little

_____

Lǚguǎn Jīnglǐ: *(juhr) (shr) (nee-duh) (jahng-dahn)* **Zhèr shì nǐde zhàngdān.**
                                                           your   bill

_____

If **nǐ** *(yoh)* **yǒu** any problems with *(shoo-zuh)* **shùzì,** just ask someone to write out the **shùzì,** so that **nǐ** can be
   have

sure you understand everything correctly,

   "**Qǐng** *(ssee-eh)* **xiě** *(choo)* **chū shùzì** *(gay)* **géi wǒ kàn.** *(ssee-eh-ssee-eh)* **Xièxie.**"
   please   write   out   for   me   to see

Practice: _____
(Please write out the number for me to see. Thank you.)

❐ **yǐ** *(yee)*	chair	
❐ **chángyǐ** *(chahng-yee)*	bench	椅
❐ **tǎngyǐ** *(tahng-yee)*	recliner	
❐ **yáoyǐ** *(yow-yee)*	rocking chair	_yǐ_
❐ **zhuànyǐ** *(jwahn-yee)*	swivel chair	

Xiànzài, let's take a break from **zhàngdān** *(jahng-dahn)* bills **hé** *(huh)* **qián** *(chee-ahn)* money and learn some fun **xīn cí.** *(sseen)* new **Nǐ** can always practice these **cí** by using your flash cards at the back of this book. Carry these flash cards in your purse, pocket, briefcase **huòzhě** knapsack and *use them!*

(ki)
kāi
open

_____

(gwahn-muhn)
guānmén
closed

_____

(dah)
dà
big

_____

(ssee-ow)
xiǎo
small

_____

(jee-ahn-kahng)
jiànkāng
healthy

_____

(beeng)
bìng
sick

_____

(how)
hǎo
good

_____

(hwhy) *(boo)* *(how)*
huài/bù hǎo
bad

_____

(ruh)
rè
hot

_____

(lung)
lěng
cold

_____

❏	**guǎn** *(gwahn)*	. . . .	place, hall
❏	**bówùguǎn** *(bwoh-woo-gwahn)*	. . . .	museum
❏	**cháguǎn** *(chah-gwahn)*	. . . .	teahouse
❏	**lǚguǎn** *(loo-we-gwahn)*	. . . .	hotel
❏	**lǐfàguǎn** *(lee-fah-gwahn)*	. . . .	barber shop

馆
guǎn

_____
_____
_____
_____

(dwahn)
duǎn _____
short

(chahng)
cháng _____
long

(mahn)
màn _____
slow

(kwhy)
kuài _____
fast

(gao)
gāo _____
tall

(I)
ǎi _____
short

(lao)
lǎo _____
old

(nee-ahn-cheeng)
niánqīng _____
young

(gway)
guì _____
expensive

(pee-ahn-yee)
piányí _____
inexpensive

(yoh-chee-ahn)
yǒuqián _____
rich

(chee-wong)
qióng _____
poor

(dwoh)
duō _____
a lot

(shao)
shǎo _____
a little

❐ **měishùguǎn** *(may-shoo-gwahn)*	art gallery	
❐ **shuǐzúguǎn** *(shway-zoo-gwahn)*	aquarium	
❐ **tǐyùguǎn** *(tee-yoo-we-gwahn)*	gymnasium	
❐ **túshūguǎn** *(too-shoo-gwahn)*	library	
❐ **zhǎnlǎnguǎn** *(jahn-lahn-gwahn)*	exhibition hall	

馆
guǎn

(juhr) *(shr)* *(sih)* *(sseen)* *(dwong-tsih)*
Zhèr shì sì ge xīn dòngcí.
four · new

(jihr-dow)
zhīdào _____
to know

(nung)
néng _____
to be able to, can

(kahn)
kàn _____
to read, look at

(yeeng-gi)
yīnggāi _____
to have to, should

Study the patterns below closely, as **nǐ** will use these **dòngcí** a lot.
verbs

(jihr-dow)
zhīdào
to know

Wǒ _____ **nà ge.**
that

(yee-dee-ahn)
Nǐ _____ **yìdiǎn Zhōngwén.**
a little

(huhn) *(dwoh)*
Tā _____ **hěn duō.**
very much

Wǒmen bù _____ **hěn duō.**

Tāmen bù _____ **.**

(nung)
néng
to be able to/can

Wǒ _____ **kàn Zhōngwén.**
read
(shwoh)
Nǐ _____ **shuō Zhōngwén.**
speak
(dwong)
Tā *néng/* _____ **dǒng Zhōngwén.**
understand

Wǒmen _____ **dǒng Yīnggwén.**

Nǐmen _____ **kàn Zhōngwén.**

(kahn)
kàn
to read/look at

Wǒ _____ **shū.**

(zah-jihr)
Nǐ _____ **zázhì.**
magazine
(meeng-sseen-pee-ahn)
Tā _____ **míngxìnpiàn.**
postcard
(bee-ow-guh)
Wǒmen _____ **biǎogé.**
form
(huhn) *(dwoh)*
Nǐmen _____ **hěn duō.**
very much

(yeeng-gi)
yīnggāi
to have to/should

Wǒ _____ **shuō Zhōngwén.**

Nǐ _____ **kàn shū.**

Tā _____ **shuō Yīngwén.**

(dwong)
Wǒmen _____ **dǒng Zhōngwén.**
understand
(bao-jihr)
Tāmen _____ **kàn bàozhǐ.**
newspaper

❑ **mǐ** *(mee)*	rice	
❑ **mǐfàn** *(mee-fahn)*	cooked rice	米 _____
❑ **mǐfěn** *(mee-fuhn)*	rice noodle	_____
❑ **mǐjiǔ** *(mee-jee-oo)*	rice wine	_____
❑ **mǐsè** *(mee-suh)*	cream-colored	*mǐ*

Notice that "**néng**," (*nung*) hé "**yīnggāi**," (*yeeng-gi*) along with "**xiǎng**" (*ssee-ahng*) can be combined with another verb.
<small>am able to</small> <small>have to</small> <small>want</small>

Wǒ xiǎng xuéxí (*ssee-yoo-eh-ssee*) **Zhōngwén.**
<small>want</small> <small>to learn</small>

Wǒ néng (*nung*) **dǒng** (*dwong*) **Zhōngwén.** (*jwong-wuhn*)
<small>can</small> <small>understand</small>

Wǒ yīnggāi kàn shū. (*yeeng-gi*)
<small>have to</small> <small>read</small>

Wǒmen xiǎng xuéxí Zhōngwén.

Wǒmen néng dǒng Zhōngwén.

Wǒmen yīnggāi kàn shū.

Wǒ shuō (*shwoh*) **Zhōngwén.** (*jwong-wuhn*)
<small>speak</small>

Wǒ néng shuō (*shwoh*) **Zhōngwén.**
<small>can</small>

Wǒ yīnggāi shuō Zhōngwén.
<small>have to</small>

Wǒ xiǎng shuō Zhōngwén.
<small>want</small>

Nǐ néng (*nung*) translate these thoughts into **Zhōngwén ma?** The answers **zài xiàbiān.** (*ssee-ah-bee-ahn*)
<small>can</small> <small>below</small>

1. I can speak French. _____

2. They have to pay now. _____

3. He wants to pay. _____

4. We don't know. _____

5. She knows very much. _____

6. I can speak a little Chinese. _____

7. I cannot understand English. _____

8. We are not able to (cannot) understand German. _____

9. I want to read the newspaper. _____

10. She reads the magazine. _____

ANSWERS

1. Wǒ néng shuō Fǎwén.
2. Tāmen xiànzài yīnggāi fù qián.
3. Tā xiǎng fù qián.
4. Wǒmen bù zhīdào.
5. Tā zhīdào hěn duō.
6. Wǒ néng shuō yìdiǎn Zhōngwén.
7. Wǒ bù dǒng Yīngwén.
8. Wǒmen bù néng dǒng Déwén.
9. Wǒ xiǎng kàn bàozhǐ.
10. Tā kàn zázhì.

74

Xiànzài, draw **xiàn** *(ssee-ahn)* lines between the opposites below. Do not forget to say them out loud. Use these **cí** every day to describe **dōngxi** *(dwong-ssee)* things **zài nǐde** *(nee-duh)* your **fángzi, nǐde xuéxiào** *(ssee-yoo-eh-ssee-ow)* school or **nǐde** your **bàngōngshì.** *(bahn-gohng-shr)* office

(gao) **gāo**

(ssee-ah) **xià**

(nee-ahn-cheeng) **niánqīng**

(chee-wong) **qióng**

(jee-ahn-kahng) **jiànkāng**

(chahng) **cháng**

(dwoh) **duō**

(how) **hǎo**

(ruh) **rè**

(zwoh) **zuǒ**

(mahn) **màn**

(gway) **guì**

(ssee-ow) **xiǎo**

(shahng) **shàng**

(I) **ǎi**

(shao) **shǎo**

(dah) **dà**

(pee-ahn-yee) **piányí**

(beeng) **bīng**

(lao) **lǎo**

(kwhy) **kuài**

(yoh) **yòu**

(lung) **lěng**

(yoh-chee-ahn) **yǒuqián**

(hwhy) **huài**

(dwahn) **duǎn**

☐ **yuè** *(yoo-eh)*	month, moon	
☐ **yuèbào** *(yoo-eh-bao)*	monthly magazine	月
☐ **yuèliang** *(yoo-eh-lee-ahng)*	moon	
☐ **yuèsè** *(yoo-eh-suh)*	moonlight	
☐ **yuèyè** *(yoo-eh-yeh)*	moonlit night	*yuè*

75

(loo-we-kuh) *(loo-wee-sseeng)*
Lǔkè Lǚxíng
traveler travels

(zwoh-tee-ahn) (dow)
Zuótiān dào Nánjīng!
yesterday to

(jeen-tee-ahn)
Jīntiān dào Shànghǎi!
today

(meeng-tee-ahn)
Míngtiān dào Běijīng!
tomorrow

(loo-we-sseeng) *(huhn)* *(rohng-yee)* *(ruhn)(doh)* *(huhn)* *(huh)*
Zài Zhōngguó, lǚxíng hěn róngyì. Zhōngguó rén dōu hěn helpful. **Zhōngguó hé**
travel very easy people all very

(may-gwoh) *(chah-boo-dwoh)* *(yee-yahng)(dah)* *(yoh)* *(huhn)*
Měiguó chàbùduō yíyàng dà. Zài Zhōngguó yǒu hěn many ways **lǚxíng:**
about same size there are very to travel

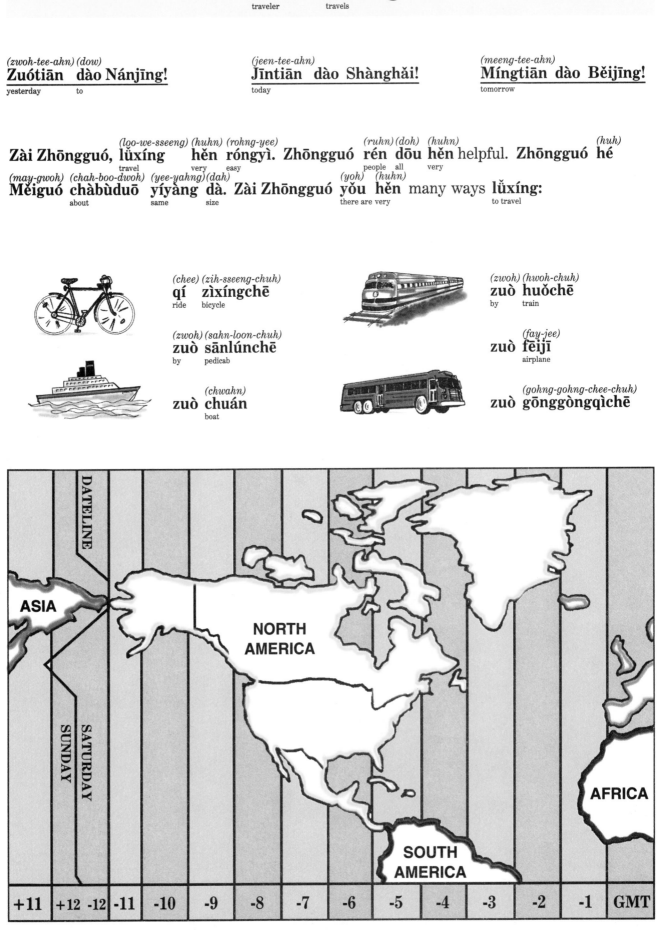

(chee) (zih-sseeng-chuh)
qí zìxíngchē
ride bicycle

(zwoh) (sahn-loon-chuh)
zuò sānlúnchē
by pedicab

(chwahn)
zuò chuán
boat

(zwoh) (hwoh-chuh)
zuò huǒchē
by train

(fay-jee)
zuò fēijī
airplane

(gohng-gohng-chee-chuh)
zuò gōnggòngqìchē

DATELINE

ASIA

NORTH
AMERICA

AFRICA

SATURDAY
SUNDAY

SOUTH
AMERICA

+11	+12	-12	-11	-10	-9	-8	-7	-6	-5	-4	-3	-2	-1	GMT

When **nǐ** are traveling, **nǐ** will want to tell others your nationality and **nǐ** will meet people from all corners of the world. Can you guess where people are from if they say one of the following? The answers are in your glossary beginning on page 108.

(woh) (tswong) (yeeng-gwoh) (lie)
Wǒ cóng Yīngguó lái. _____

(yee-dah-lee)
Wǒ cóng Yìdàlì lái. _____

(may-gwoh)
Wǒ cóng Měiguó lái. _____

(ssee-bahn-yah)
Wǒ cóng Xībānyá lái. _____

(ow-dah-lee-yah)
Wǒ cóng Āodàlìyà lái. _____

(lao-woh)
Wǒ cóng Lǎowō lái. _____

(huh-lahn)
Wǒ cóng Hélán lái. _____

(yoo-eh-nahn)
Wǒ cóng Yuènán lái. _____

(nwoh-way)
Wǒ cóng Nuówēi lái. _____

(tswong) (yeen-doo-nee-ssee-yah) (lie)
Wǒmen cóng Yìndùníxīyà lái. _____

(duh-gwoh)
Wǒmen cóng Déguó lái. _____

(muhng-goo)
Wǒmen cóng Měnggǔ lái. _____

(ree-buhn)
Wǒmen cóng Rìběn lái. _____

(sseen-ssee-lahn)
Tā cóng Xīnxīlán lái. _____

(yeen-doo)
Tā cóng Yìndù lái. _____

(dahn-my)
Tā cóng Dānmài lái. _____

(tie-gwoh)
Tā cóng Tàiguó lái. _____

(jee-ah-nah-dah)
Tā cóng Jiānádà lái. _____

EUROPE

ASIA

AFRICA

DATELINE

SATURDAY SUNDAY

| -1 | GMT | +1 | +2 | +3 | +4 | +5 | +6 | +7 | +8 | +9 | +10 | +11 | +12 -12 |

Due to the amount of *(why-gwoh)* **wàiguó** visitors in **Zhōngguó,** you will see many "travel" **cí.** Practice
foreign

saying the following **cí** many times. **Nǐ** will see them often.

(ssee-ahng)
xiàng _____
lane

(loo-we-sseeng) (shuh)
lǚxíng shè _____
travel   agent

(loo-we-kuh)
lǚkè _____
passenger, traveler

(seeng-lee)
xínglǐ _____
luggage, baggage

(jee-eh)
jiē _____
street

(sseeng-lee) (chuh)
xínglǐ chē _____
baggage   cart

(dah-dow)
dàdào _____
boulevard

(ruhn-sseeng-dow)
rénxíngdào _____
sidewalk

Xiàbiān shì four **cí** which should help you whenever you travel in and out of the country.

(wuhn-jee-ahn)	*(hoo-jow)*	*(chee-ahn-jung)*	*(jee-ahn-kahng) (jung-meeng)*	*(shoo)*
wénjiàn	**hùzhào**	**qiānzhèng**	**jiànkāng zhèngmíng**	**shū**
documents	passport	visa	health certificate	

Zhèr shì some basic signs which **nǐ** *(yuh)* **yě** should learn to recognize quickly.
also

(roo-koh)
rùkǒu _____
entrance

(choo-koh)
chūkǒu _____
exit

Rùkǒu 入口

Chūkǒu 出口

(jeen) (jihr) (twong) (sseeng)
jìn zhǐ tōng xíng _____
no trespassing

(tie-peeng) (muhn)
tàipíng mén _____
emergency gate

(jeen) (jihr) (jow-ssee-ahng)
jìn zhǐ zhàoxiàng _____
no photos allowed

(chee-eh) (woo) (roo-nay)
qiè wù rùnèi _____
keep out

Tuī 推

Lā 拉

(tway)
tuī _____
push (doors)

(lah)
lā _____
pull (doors)

❑ **èryuè** *(ur-yoo-eh)* . . . . February		_____
❑ **jiǔyuè** *(jee-oo-yoo-eh)* . . . . September	**月**	_____
❑ **liùyuè** *(lee-oo-yoo-eh)* . . . . June		_____
❑ **shíyīyuè** *(shr-yee-yoo-eh)* . . . . November		_____
❑ **sìyuè** *(sih-yoo-eh)* . . . . April	*yuè*	_____

Let's learn the basic travel verbs. Take out a piece of paper and make up your own sentences with these **xīn cí.** Follow the same pattern **nǐ** have in previous Steps.

(fay)
fēi _____
to fly

(loo-we-sseeng)
lǔxíng _____
to travel

(dow)
dào _____
to arrive

(hwahn) *(chuh)*
huàn chē _____
to transfer (vehicles)

(ki)
kāi _____
to leave, depart

(shwoh-shr)
shōushi _____
to pack

(deeng)
dìng _____
to book, reserve

(zwoh)
zuò _____
to sit, ride in

Zhèr are more **xīn cí** for your trip.
(sseen)
new

(fay-jee-chahng)
fēijīchǎng
airport

(hwoh-chuh) *(yoo-eh-tie)*
huǒchē yuètái
train   platform

_____

_____

(shr-jee-ahn) *(bee-ow)*
shíjiān biǎo
time   schedule

(hwoh-chuh) *(zwong)* *(jahn)*
huǒchē zǒng zhàn
train   main   station

Cóng Shànghǎi dào Nánjīng		
Kāi	Huǒchē	Dào
08:30	Kuàichē	10:30
11:10	Kuàichē	13:10
13:25	Pǔtōngchē	19:25
16:15	Pǔtōngchē	22:15

_____

_____

☐ **shí** (*shr*) . . . . stone, rock
☐ **shídiāo** (*shr-dee-ow*) . . . . carved stone
☐ **shíkuài** (*shr-kwhy*) . . . . boulder
☐ **shímò** (*shr-mwoh*) . . . . graphite
☐ **shíyīng** (*shr-yeeng*) . . . . quartz

石
shí

_____

_____

_____

_____

_____

With **zhè xiē** *(juh) (ssee-eh)* **dòngcí,** *(dwong-tsih)* **nǐ** are ready for any **lǚxíng** *(loo-we-sseeng)* anywhere. **Nǐ** should have no problems
these several

with these verbs, just remember the basic "plug-in" formula **nǐ** have already learned. Use that

knowledge to translate the following thoughts into **Zhōngwén.** The answers **zài xiàbiān.** *(ssee-ah-bee-ahn)*

1. I fly to Nanjing. _____

2. I pack tomorrow. _____

3. We travel to Kunming. _____

4. He sits in the airplane. _____

5. She books the flight to go to America. _____

6. They travel to Hangzhou. _____

7. Where is the train to Xi'an? _____

8. How can we fly to Japan? _____

Zhèr are some **zhòngyàode cí** *(jwong-yow-duh)* for the **lǚke.** *(loo-we-kuh)*
important   traveler

Cóng Shànghǎi dào Nánjīng		
Kāi	Huǒchē	Dào
08:30	Kuàichē	10:30
11:10	Kuàichē	13:10
13:25	Pǔtōngchē	19:25
16:15	Pǔtōngchē	22:15

(yoh-ruhn)
yǒurén _____
occupied

(dway-hwahn) (choo)
duìhuàn chù _____
money-exchange office

(chuh-ssee-ahng)
chēxiāng _____
compartment

(zwoh-way)
zuòwèi _____
seat

(dow)
dào _____
to arrive, arrival

(ki)
kāi _____
to depart, departure

(gwoh-why)
guówài _____
international

(gwoh-nay)
guónèi _____
domestic

ANSWERS

1. **Wǒ zuò fēijī dào Nánjīng.**
2. **Wǒ míngtiān shōushí xíngli.**
3. **Wǒmen qù Kūnmíng lǚxíng.**
4. **Tā zuò zài fēijī lǐ.**
5. **Tā dìng qù Měiguó de jīpiào.**
6. **Tāmen qù Hángzhōu lǚxíng.**
7. **Dào Xī'ān qù de huǒchē zài nǎr?**
8. **Wǒmen zěnme fēi dào Rìběn?**

Increase your travel **cí** by writing out the *(ssee-ah-bee-ahn-duh)* **xiàbiānde** below **cí** and practicing the sample sentences out loud. Substitute your destination and practice using different numbers.

(dow)
dào _____
to
                     Dào Shànghǎi de huǒchē zài nǎr?

(shoh-pee-ow) *(choo)*
shòupiào chù _____
ticket   office
                     Shòupiào chù zài nǎr?

(shr-woo) *(jow-leeng)*
shīwù zhāolǐng _____
lost-and-found office
                     Shīwù zhāolǐng zài nǎr?

(sseeng-lee) *(chuh)*
xínglǐ chē *Nǎr yǒu xínglǐ chē? Nǎr yǒu xínglǐ chē?*
baggage   cart
                     Nǎr yǒu xínglǐ chē?

(tee-eh-gway)
tiěguǐ _____
track
                     Dìqī tiáo tiěguǐ zài nǎr?
                     seventh (M)

(yoo-eh-tie)
yuètái _____
platform
                     Dìbā yuètái zài nǎr?
                     eighth

(dway-hwahn) *(choo)*
duìhuàn chù _____
money-exchange office
                     Nǎr yǒu duìhuàn chù?

(gway-tie)
guìtái _____
counter
                     Bā hào guìtái zài nǎr?

(hoh-chuh-shr)
hòuchēshì _____
waiting room
                     Hòuchēshì zài nǎr?

(tsahn-chuh)
cānchē _____
dining car
                     Zhè ge huǒchē yǒu cānchē ma?

(woh-poo)
wòpù _____
sleeping car
                     Zhè ge huǒchē yǒu wòpù ma?

(tahng-yee)
tǎngyǐ _____
reclining car
                     Zhè ge huǒchē yǒu tǎngyǐ ma?

___(when)___ *(fay-jee)* **Fēijī** ___(when)___ *(ki)* **kāi?**
airplane

___(what)___ **Nà shì** ___(what)___ **?**

☐	**bǎoshí** *(bao-shr)*	gem	
☐	**hǎi lán bǎoshí** *(hi)(lahn)(bao-shr)*	aquamarine	
☐	**hóng bǎoshí** *(hohng)(bao-shr)*	ruby	石
☐	**lán bǎoshí** *(lahn)(bao-shr)*	sapphire	*shí*
☐	**zuànshí** *(zwahn-shr)*	diamond	

(ssee-ah-bee-ahn-duh) *(nung)* *(kahn)*
Xiàbiānde nǐ néng kàn ma?
can read

Xiànzài nǐ zuò zài fēi qù Zhōngguó
(zwoh) *(fay)* *(choo)*
sit fly

de fēijī shàng. Nǐ yǒu le piào,
(fay-jee) *(pee-ow)*
airplane on ticket

qián hé hùzhào. Nǐ dài le nǐde
(chee-ahn) *(hoo-jow)* *(die)* *(nee-duh)*
money passport bring your

xiāngzi. Xiànzài nǐ shì yí ge lǚkè.
(ssee-ahng-zuh) *(shr)* *(loo-we-kuh)*
suitcase are traveler

Nǐ shísì xiǎoshí hòu zài Zhōngguó
(shr-sih) *(ssee-ow-shr)* *(hoh)*
fourteen hours after

jiàngluò.
(jee-ahng-lwoh)
land

Yí lù píng ān!
(loo) *(peeng)* *(ahn)*
safe and peaceful journey

Zhōngguó huǒchē come in many shapes, sizes and speeds. **Zài Zhōngguó**, there are **pǔtōngchē,**
(poo-tohng-chuh)
ordinary trains

kuàichē hé tèbié kuàichē. Some **huǒchē yǒu cānchē.** Some **huǒchē yǒu wòpù.** Some
(kwhy-chuh) *(tuh-bee-uh)* *(kwhy-chuh)* *(yoh)* *(tsahn-chuh)* *(woh-poo)*
fast trains special fast trains have dining car sleeping car

huǒchē yǒu tǎngyǐ. All this will be indicated on the **shíjiān biǎo,** but remember, **nǐ zhīdào**
(tahng-yee) *(shr-jee-ahn)* *(bee-ow)* *(jihr-dow)*
reclining car time schedule know

zěnme wèn zhè xiē wèntí.
(zuhn-muh) *(wuhn)* *(juh)* *(ssee-eh)*
how to ask these

❒ **hǎo** *(how)*	good	
❒ **hǎochī** *(how-chr)*	delicious	
❒ **hǎochù** *(how-choo)*	benefit	好
❒ **hǎogǎn** *(how-gahn)*	good impression	*hǎo*
❒ **hǎoyì** *(how-yee)*	goodwill	

Knowing these travel **cí** will make your holiday twice as enjoyable and at least three times as easy. Review these **cí** by doing the crossword puzzle below. Drill yourself on this Step by selecting other destinations and ask your own **wèntí** about **huǒchē,** *(hwoh-chuh)* **gōnggòngqìchē** *(gohng-gohng-chee-chuh)* **huòzhě** **fēijī** *(fay-jee)* that go there. Select more **xīn cí** from your **cídiǎn** *(tsih-dee-ahn)* and practice asking **wèntí** beginning
airplanes   dictionary
with **nǎr, shénme shíhou** and **duōshao qián.**

ACROSS

4. sleeping car
6. to book, reserve
7. to arrive, to
8. where
10. international
11. language
12. exit
14. pedicab
15. airport
19. train
20. main station
22. traveler, passenger
25. luggage, baggage
27. time schedule
28. very
29. counter

DOWN

1. documents
2. to pay
3. ticket
5. dining car
6. money-exchange office
7. map
9. entrance
12. compartment
13. emergency gate
14. lost-and-found office
16. passport
17. to know
18. airplane
21. to travel
23. fast
24. reclining car
26. boat

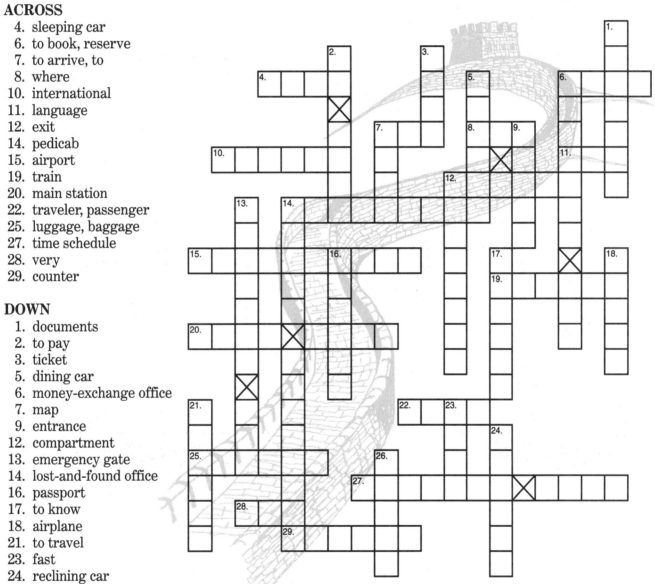

The Great Wall, or as it is known in Chinese — **"Chángchéng,"** was originally constructed during the Qin Dynasty (221-207 B.C.). Over time additional walls were linked to it. The estimates of its exact length range from 1,560 miles to over 3,000 miles.

❑ **hǎohàn** *(how-hahn)* . . . . wise man, hero _____
❑ **hǎotīng** *(how-teeng)* . . . . pleasant to the ear _____
❑ **hǎoxiào** *(how-ssee-ow)* . . . . funny _____
❑ **hǎokàn** *(how-kahn)* . . . . good-looking _____
❑ **hǎoyùn** *(how-yoon)* . . . . good fortune   好   _____
                                                                          hǎo

83

What about inquiring about **jiàqián?** *(jee-ah-chee-ahn)* **Nǐ néng wèn zhè ge wèntí.** *(nung) (wuhn)*
prices · can · ask

Cóng Shànghǎi dào Běijīng duōshao qián? _____
(tswong) from · *(dow)* to · *(dwoh-shao)* how much · *(chee-ahn)* money

dānchéng _____
(dahn-chuhng) one-way

láihuí _____
(lie-hway) round-trip

Cóng Shànghǎi dào Nánjīng duōshao qián? _____
(dwoh-shao) *(chee-ahn)*

Dānchéng háishì láihuí? _____
(dahn-chuhng) one-way · *(hi-shr)* or · *(lie-hway)* round-trip

Nǐ yě néng wèn: *(yeh) (nung) (wuhn)* **Shénme shíhou kāi?** *(shun-muh) (shr-hoh) (ki)*   **Shénme shíhou dào?** *(dow)*
also · can · ask   what · time · depart   arrive

Qù Guǎngzhōu de huǒchē shénme shíhou kāi? _____
(chee-oo) to · *(hwoh-chuh)* train · *(ki)* departs

Qù Shànghǎi de fēijī shénme shíhou kāi? _____
(fay-jee) airplane

Huǒchē shénme shíhou dào Xī'ān? _____
(dow) arrives

Fēijī shénme shíhou dào Běijīng? _____

Nǐ have just arrived in **Zhōngguó. Xiànzài nǐ zài huǒchē zhàn. Nǐ yào qù nǎr? Hǎo,**
(jahn) are (at) · station · *(yow)* want · *(chee-oo)* to go · *(how)* where · well

tell that to the **shòupiàoyuán** at the **guìtái.**
(shoh-pee-ow-yoo-ahn) ticket seller · *(gway-tie)* counter

Wǒ xiǎng dào Hángzhōu qù. _____
(ssee-ahng) want · to · *(chee-oo)* to go

Dào Hángzhōu de chē shénme shíhou kāi? _____
(dow) to · *(chuh)* · *(shr-hoh)* · *(ki)*

Dào Hángzhōu de piào duōshao qián? _____
(pee-ow) ticket · *(dwoh-shao)* how much · *(chee-ahn)* money

Wǒ xiǎng yào yì zhāng piào. _____
would like · (M) · *(pee-ow)* ticket

84

Xiànzài that **nǐ** know the words essential for traveling **zài Zhōngguó**, what are some specialty items **nǐ** might go in search of?

(sih)
sī
silk

(jee-nee-ahn-peen)
jìniànpǐn
souvenirs

(gohng-yee-peen)
gōngyìpǐn
artworks

(joo-bao)
zhūbǎo
jewelry

(dee-ow-kuh)
diāokè
carvings

(chah-joo)
chájù
tea service

Consider using CHINESE *a language map*™ as well. CHINESE *a language map*™ is the perfect companion for your travels when **nǐ** may not wish to take along this book. Each section focuses on essentials for your journey. Your *Language Map*™ is not meant to replace learning
(jwong-wuhn)
Zhōngwén, but will help you in the event **nǐ** forget something and need a little bit of help.

- ❑ **chá** *(chah)* . . . . tea
- ❑ **chábēi** *(chah-bay)* . . . . tea cup
- ❑ **chádiǎn** *(chah-dee-ahn)* . . . . light meal
- ❑ **cháguǎn** *(chah-gwahn)* . . . . teahouse
- ❑ **cháhuì** *(chah-hway)* . . . . tea party

茶
chá

(tsi-dahn)
Càidān
menu

Xiànzài nǐ zài Zhōngguó de lǚguǎn *(loo-we-gwahn)* le. Nǐ are hungry. Nǐ xiǎng yào chīfàn *(chr-fahn)*. Hǎo *(how)*
hotel / to eat meal / good

fànguǎn zài nǎr? First of all, yǒu *(yoh)* hěn *(huhn)* duō *(dwoh)* chīfàn *(chr-fahn)* de dìfāng *(dee-fahng)*. Let's learn them.
there are very / many / to eat meal / places

lǚguǎn *(loo-we-gwahn)* **de chāntīng** *(chahn-teeng)* _____
a café in a hotel that serves a variety of **Zhōngguó**
as well as **Měiguó** dishes

xiǎo *(ssee-ow)* **chīdiàn** *(chr-dee-ahn)* _____
a snack shop, usually open for breakfast, lunch and dinner

miàn *(mee-ahn)* **guǎn** *(gwahn)* _____
a noodle shop that provides a variety of noodle dishes

jiǔ *(jee-oo)* **guǎn** *(gwahn)* _____
a tavern that has a limited menu but some specialties

fànguǎn *(fahn-gwahn)* _____
a restaurant that serves a variety of meals, depending upon
the province you are visiting

If **nǐ** look around you in a **Zhōngguó fànguǎn**, **nǐ** will see that **Zhōngguó rén** *(ruhn)* uses two basic
person

eating utensils: 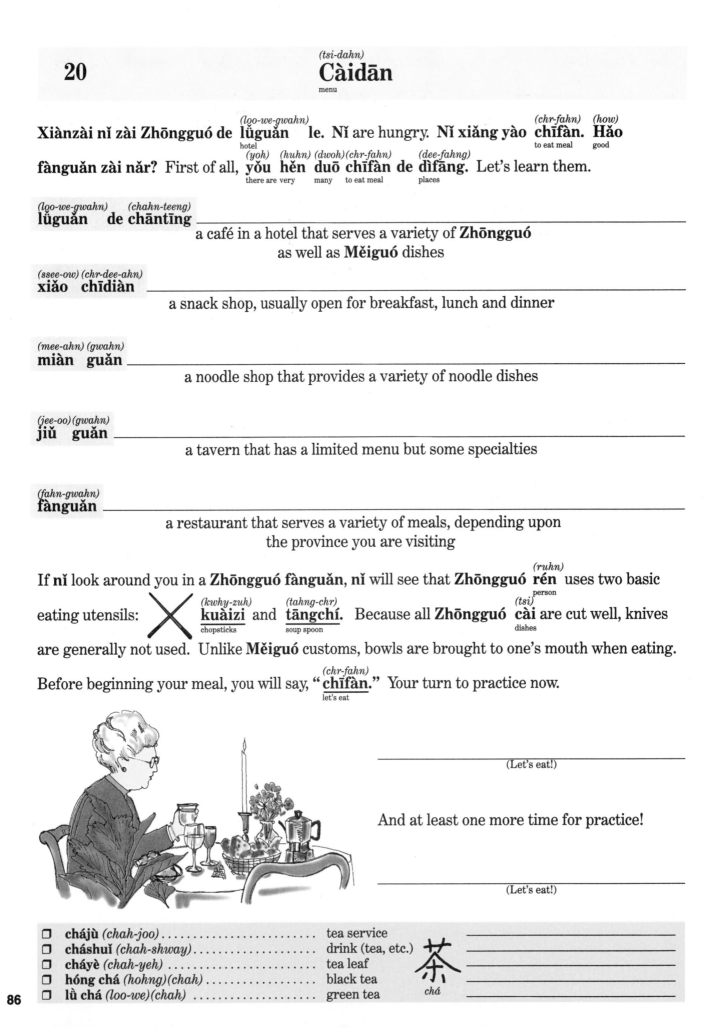 **kuàizi** *(kwhy-zuh)* and **tāngchí** *(tahng-chr)*. Because all **Zhōngguó cài** *(tsi)* are cut well, knives
chopsticks / soup spoon / dishes

are generally not used. Unlike **Měiguó** customs, bowls are brought to one's mouth when eating.

Before beginning your meal, you will say, "**chīfàn** *(chr-fahn)*." Your turn to practice now.
let's eat

_____
(Let's eat!)

And at least one more time for practice!

_____
(Let's eat!)

☐ **chájù** *(chah-joo)*	tea service	_____
☐ **cháshuǐ** *(chah-shway)*	drink (tea, etc.)	茶 _____
☐ **cháyè** *(chah-yeh)*	tea leaf	_____
☐ **hóng chá** *(hohng)(chah)*	black tea	_____
☐ **lǜ chá** *(loo-we)(chah)*	green tea	*chá* _____

Start imagining now all the new taste treats you will experience abroad. Try all of the different

types of eating establishments mentioned on the previous page. Experiment. **Nǐ** may share a

(jwoh-zuh)
zhuōzi with others, which is a common and pleasant custom in **Zhōngguó**. If **nǐ kànjiàn** a vacant
table   *(kahn-jee-ahn)*
                                                                                                                              see

(yee-zuh)   *(jwoh-zuh)*   *(ssee-ahn-shuhng) (juhr)   (ruhn)*
yǐzi, just be sure to first ask those sitting at the **zhuōzi**, "**Xiānshēng, zhèr yǒu rén ma?**"
chair   sir   there has person

(ssee-oo-yow)   *(tsi-dahn)*
If **nǐ xūyào   yí ge càidān,** catch the attention
      need   menu
                (foo-woo-yoo-ahn)
of the **fúwùyuán** saying,
        service person

> *(ssee-ahn-shuhng)*   *(tsi-dahn)*
> "**Xiānshēng, qǐng gěi wǒ càidān.**"
>   menu

_____
(Sir, I would like a menu.)

(tsi-dahn)   *(jihr-dow)*
Zhōngguó fànguǎn post their **càidān** outside. Always read it before entering so **nǐ zhīdào**
                                  menu   know
                            (jee-ah-chee-ahn)
what type of meals and **jiàqián   nǐ** will encounter inside. Most **fànguǎn** will also write the
                          prices

                                                                              (muhn)
special meal of the day on a blackboard just inside the **mén.** The meal of the day is always
                                                          door

seasonal and often consists of seafood or vegetables.

❐ **diàn** *(dee-ahn)*	store, shop	
❐ **diànyuán** *(dee-ahn-yoo-ahn)*	store clerk	
❐ **diànzhǔ** *(dee-ahn-joo)*	storekeeper	店
❐ **gǔdǒng diàn** *(goo-dwong)(dee-ahn)*	antique shop	
❐ **huā/huār diàn** *(hwah/hwahr)(dee-ahn)*	florist shop	*diàn*

Zài Zhōngguó, *(yoh)* **yǒu** *(sahn)* **sān ge** *(jwong-yow-duh)* **zhòngyàode** meals to enjoy every day, plus *(ssee-ah-woo-duh)* **xiàwǔde** snacks **hé**
there are *three* *important* *afternoon*

(wahn-shahng-duh)
wǎnshàngde snacks.
evening

(zow-fahn)
zǎofàn _____
breakfast

Zài lǚguǎn, nǐ may eat **zǎofàn** between **liù diǎn** *(dee-ahn)* and **bā diǎn.**
o'clock

Be sure to check the schedule before you retire for the night.

(woo-fahn)
wǔfàn _____
mid-day meal

generally served from 11:30 to 14:30

(wahn-fahn)
wǎnfàn _____
evening meal

generally served from 18:00 to 20:30 and sometimes later;

after 21:00, only snacks will be served.

Xiànzài, for a preview of delights to come . . . At the back of this **shū, nǐ** will find a sample

(tsi-dahn) *(jeen-tee-ahn)*
càidān. Read it **jīntiān** and learn the **xīn cí.** When **nǐ** are ready to leave on your trip, cut out
today

the **càidān,** fold it, **hé** carry it in your pocket, wallet **huòzhě** purse. Before you go, how do **nǐ** say

these **sān** phrases which are so very important for the hungry traveler?

Sir, is this space vacant (is there a person here)? _____

Sir, I would like the menu. _____

Let's eat! _____

(chr) *(yoo-we)*
_____ **chī yú?**   _____ **hē jiǔ?**
(who)   *(who)*
          eats *fish*   *drinks*

(dow)
_____ (who)   _____ **lǚxíng dào Shànghǎi?**
                    (who)   *to*

❏ **lǐfà diàn** *(lee-fah)(dee-ahn)*	hairdresser's	
❏ **ròu diàn** *(roh)(dee-ahn)*	butcher shop	
❏ **shū diàn** *(shoo)(dee-ahn)*	bookstore	店
❏ **yào diàn** *(yow)(dee-ahn)*	pharmacy	*diàn*
❏ **xié diàn** *(ssee-eh)(dee-ahn)*	shoe store	

(tsi-dahn)

Càidān below has the main categories **nǐ** will find in most restaurants. Learn them **jīntiān** so that **nǐ** will easily recognize them when you dine **zài Zhōngguó.** Be sure to write the words in the blanks below.

(tsi-dahn)
Càidān

(lung-pahn)
lěngpán
appetizers

_____

(tahng)
tāng
soups

_____

(dahn)
dàn
eggs

_____

(hi-ssee-ahn)
hǎixiān
seafood

_____

(nee-oo-roh)
niúròu
beef

_____

(yah)
yā
duck

_____

(jee)
jī
chicken

_____

(joo-roh)
zhūròu
pork

_____

(shway-gwoh)
shuǐguǒ
fruit

_____

(cheeng-tsi)
qīngcài
green vegetables

_____

(mee-ahn) (fahn)
miàn fàn
noodles and rice

_____

(tee-ahn-dee-ahn)
tiándiǎn
dessert

_____

(yeen-lee-ow)
yǐnliào
beverages

_____

Learning the following should help you to identify what kind of meat **nǐ** have ordered and **zěnme** it will be prepared.

❑	**niúròu** *(nee-oo-roh)*	beef	_____
❑	**jī** *(jee)*	chicken	_____
❑	**zhūròu** *(joo-roh)*	pork	_____
❑	**yángròu** *(yahng-roh)*	mutton	_____

Nǐ néng *(nung)* generally order **qīngcài** *(cheeng-tsi)* with your meal, as well as **miàn** *(mee-ahn)* or **fàn** *(fahn)*. One **tiān** at a
can *green vegetables* *noodles* *rice*
càichǎng *(tsi-chahng)* will teach **nǐ** the **míngzì** of different kinds of **cài** *(tsi)* **hé shuǐguǒ,** *(shway-gwoh)* plus it will be a
market *vegetables* *fruit*

delightful experience for **nǐ**. **Nǐ néng** *(nung)* always consult your menu guide at the back of this **shū** if

nǐ forget the **zhèngquède** *(jung-choo-eh-duh)* **míngzì**. **Xiànzài nǐ** have decided what **nǐ xiǎng yào chī** *(chr)* and
correct *would like* *to eat*
fúwùyuán *(foo-woo-yoo-ahn)* **lái** *(lie)* **le.**
service person *comes*

Xiānshēng, qǐng gěi wǒ càidān.

Hē shénme?

Qǐng gěi wǒ yì bēi jiǔ.

Don't forget that **Zhōngguó** dishes are regional and that various provinces have their own

specialties. **Nǐ** would not want to miss out on the following specialties.

zòngzi *(zwong-zuh)*
stuffed sweet rice wrapped with bamboo leaves

tāngyuán *(tahng-yoo-ahn)*
sweet rice-flour ball

chūnjuǎn *(choon-joo-ahn)*
pastry filled with a savory mixture of vegetables and meat (spring roll)

xiāròu *(ssee-ah-roh)* **hún tun** *(hoon) (toon)*
shrimp and vegetables in a wrapper, boiled

Most **fànguǎn** also offer **náshǒucài,** *(nah-shoh-tsi)* which are the chef's special dishes. Because it is a custom

in **Zhōngguó** to share all the dishes which one's party has ordered, make sure you know the size

of the dish before you order it. The dishes will be marked in the **càidān** *(tsi-dahn)* as

Small 小 Medium 中 Large 大

☐ **yā** *(yah)* . . . . duck _____
☐ **yú** *(yoo-we)* . . . . fish _____
☐ **jīdàn** *(jee-dahn)* . . . . eggs _____
☐ **zhà** *(jah)* . . . . deep-fried _____
☐ **shāo** *(shao)* . . . . roasted _____

Zhèr shì *(juhr)* an example of what **nǐ** might select for your evening meal. Using your menu guide on
this
pages 117 and 118, as well as what **nǐ** have learned in this Step, fill in the blanks *in English*
with what **nǐ** believe your **fúwùyuán** *(foo-woo-yoo-uhn)* will bring you. The answers **zài xiàbiān.** *(ssee-ah-bee-ahn)*

Lěngpán
Yóu bào xiā

_____

Tāng
Dàn huā tāng

_____

Niúròu
Chǎo niúròu sī, bái fàn

_____

Tiándiǎn
Básī píngguǒ

_____

(when)   (how)   (why)

Xiànzài is a good time for a quick review. Draw lines between the matching **Yīngwén** and **Zhōngwén cí** below.

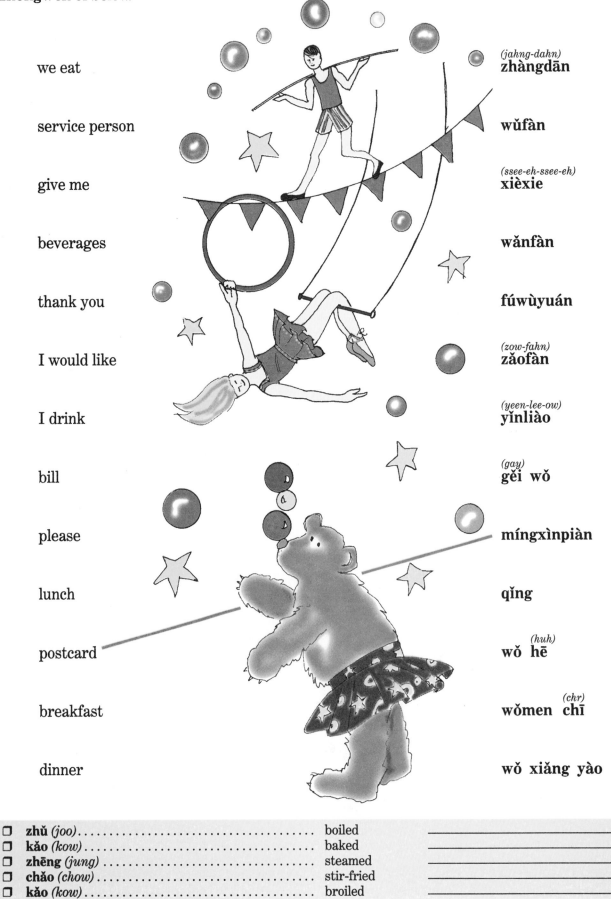

we eat

service person

give me

beverages

thank you

I would like

I drink

bill

please

lunch

postcard

breakfast

dinner

(jahng-dahn)
zhàngdān

wǔfàn

(ssee-eh-ssee-eh)
xièxie

wǎnfàn

fúwùyuán

(zow-fahn)
zǎofàn

(yeen-lee-ow)
yǐnliào

(gay)
gěi wǒ

míngxìnpiàn

qǐng

(huh)
wǒ hē

(chr)
wǒmen chī

wǒ xiǎng yào

☐ **zhǔ** *(joo)*..	boiled	_____
☐ **kǎo** *(kow)*..	baked	_____
☐ **zhēng** *(jung)*....................................	steamed	_____
☐ **chǎo** *(chow)*....................................	stir-fried	_____
☐ **kǎo** *(kow)*..	broiled	_____

21

(dee-ahn-hwah)
Diànhuà
telephone

Zài Zhōngguó, what is different about the **diànhuà?** *(dee-ahn-hwah)* Well, **nǐ** never notice such things until **nǐ** want to use them. **Diànhuà** allow you to make reservations for a **lǚguǎn,** **mǎi** **xìpiào** *(my)* *(ssee-pee-ow)* **hé**
hotel   buy   theater tickets

fēijīpiào, *(fay-jee-pee-ow)* contact **nǐde** *(nee-duh)* **péngyou,** *(pung-yoh)* check on the hours of a **bówùguǎn,** call a **chūzūchē,** *(choo-zoo-chuh)* make
airplane tickets   your   friends   museum

emergency calls and a lot of other things that **wǒmen** do **tiāntiān.** *(tee-ahn-tee-ahn)* It also gives you a certain
everyday

amount of freedom when **nǐ** can make your own calls.

Zài Zhōngguó many **jiālǐ** *(jee-ah-lee)* **yǒu diànhuà.** Depending upon where your travels take you, **nǐ**
homes (inside)   have

may need to find a **gōngyòng diànhuà. Zài** *(gohng-yohng)*
public

yóujú *(yoh-joo-we)* **yǒu** **gōngyòng diànhuà.** *(gohng-yohng)* **Fēijīchǎng** *(fay-jee-chahng)*
post office   there are public   airports

hé a few of the large shopping centers also

yǒu diànhuà tíng.
booths

So, let's learn **zěnme** *(zuhn-muh)* to operate the
how

diànhuà. The instructions can look

complicated, but remember, **nǐ** can do

this. Many **diànhuà** use **diànhuà kǎ.** *(kah)*
telephone   cards

Nǐ néng *(nung)* buy these at the post office. Ready?
can

Well, before you turn the page it would be a

good idea to go back and review all your

numbers one more time.

To dial from the United States to most other countries **nǐ** need that country's international area

code. Your **diànhuà bù** *(boo)* at home should have a listing of international area codes.
telephone book

Zhèr shì some very useful words built around the word **"diànhuà."**		_____
☐ **gōngyòng diànhuà** *(gohng-yohng)(dee-ahn-hwah)*	public telephone	_____
☐ **diànhuà tíng** *(dee-ahn-hwah)(teeng)*	telephone booth	_____
☐ **diànhuà bù** *(dee-ahn-hwah)(boo)*	telephone book/register	_____
☐ **běndì diànhuà** *(buhn-dee)(dee-ahn-hwah)*	local telephone call	_____

When **nǐ** leave your contact numbers with friends, family **hé** business colleagues, **nǐ** should include your destination's country code **hé** city code whenever possible . For example,

City Codes		City Codes	
Quǎngzhōu	20	Běijīng	10
Xī'ān	29	Shànghǎi	21
Wūlǔmùqí	991	Tiānjīn	22
Hángzhōu	571	Kūnmíng	871
Wǔhàn	27	Lāsà	891

The country code for **Zhōngguó** is — 86 —

To call from one city to another **zài Zhōngguó, nǐ** may place it through your **lǚguǎn** service desk or by using a **diànhuà kǎ** (kah) in a special card telephone. **Nǐ** know how to say: "**Wǒ xiǎng yào dǎ** (make) **diànhuà dào** (dow) **Běijīng.**" or "**Wǒ xiǎng yào dǎ diànhuà dào Nánjīng.**"

telephone card

Now you try it: _____

(I would like to call . . .)

When answering the **diànhuà, nǐ** pick up the **tīngtǒng** (teeng-tohng) and say,

receiver

> "**Wèi. Nǐnhǎo.**"
> (way) (neen-how)
> hey hello

Zhōngguó rén usually say, "**Zàijiàn,**" (zi-jee-ahn) when ending a **diànhuàde** (dee-ahn-hwah-duh) **duìhuà** (dway-hwah) even though it

good-bye   conversation

actually means "see you again." Your turn – _____

(good-bye)

Also, if **nǐ** are told "**Yǒu rén shuōhuà,**" (yoh) (ruhn) (shwoh-hwah) don't be surprised — it simply means the line is occupied.

there is person speaking

Don't forget that **nǐ néng** (nung) ask . . .

can

Dǎ chángtú (chahng-too) **diànhuà dào** (dow) **Měiguó duōshao qián?** _____

make long-distance   to U.S.A.

Dǎ chángtú diànhuà dào Jiānádà (jee-ah-nah-dah) **duōshao qián?** _____

Canada

Zhèr shì some emergency telephone numbers.
- ☐ **jǐngchá** (jeeng-chah) . . . . police   110 _____
- ☐ **huǒ** (hwoh) . . . . fire   119 _____
- ☐ **běndì cháhàotái** (buhn-dee)(chah-how-tie) . . . . local directory assistance   114 _____
- ☐ **chángtú cháhàotái** (chahng-too)(chah-how-tie) . . . . long-distance assistance   113 _____

Zhèr shì some sample sentences for the **diànhuà.** Write them in the blanks to the right.

Wǒ xiǎng yào dǎ diànhuà dào San Francisco. _____

Wǒ xiǎng yào dǎ diànhuà dào *(fay-jee-chahng)* **fēijīchǎng.** _____
airport

Wǒ xiǎng yào dǎ diànhuà dào " *(jeen)* *(hi)* **Jīn Hǎi Fànguǎn."** _____
golden   sea

(woh-duh)
Wǒde diànhuà shì Běijīng, 6765-8974. _____
my

(nee-duh)   *(how)*
Nǐde diànhuà duōshao hào? _____
your   number

Lǚguǎn diànhuà duōshao hào? _____

Christina: *(way)* *(neen-how)* **Wěi. Nǐnhǎo. Qǐng** *(jee-ow)* **jiào Lǐ Sǐ tīng diànhuà.**
                                                                              call   listen to

_____

Operator: *(yoh)* *(ruhn)* *(shwoh-hwah)* **Yǒu rén shuōhuà.**

_____

Christina: **Wǒ** *(jihr)* **zhǐ shuō yìdiǎn Zhōngwén. Qǐng nǐ** *(mahn)* *(mahn)* **màn man shuō.**
                      only   a little   slowly

_____

Operator: **Duìbùqǐ. Yǒu rén shuōhuà.**

_____

Christina: **Xièxie.** *(zi-jee-ahn)* **Zàijiàn.**

_____

When speaking to someone in a foreign language, it is most helpful if you look at the person,

speak **hěn** slowly and distinctly. **Nǐ** don't need to **raise** your voice, just speak clearly.

Zhèr shì countries **nǐ** may wish to call.
- ❏ **Āodàlìyá** *(ow-dah-lee-yah)* . . . . Australia _____
- ❏ **Āodìlì** *(ow-dee-lee)* . . . . Austria _____
- ❏ **Bǐlìshí** *(bee-lee-shr)* . . . . Belgium _____
- ❏ **Jiānádà** *(jee-ah-nah-dah)* . . . . Canada _____

95

22

车 *chē*   *(chuh)* **Chē**   车 *chē*

vehicles

An excellent means of transportation is the **dìtiě**. *(dee-tee-eh)* However, most **Zhōngguó rén** travel by

diànchē *(dee-ahn-chuh)* **huòzhě gōnggòngqìchē** *(gohng-gohng-chee-chuh)*. **Zài Zhōngguó, gōnggòngqìchē** are **chángcháng** *(chahng-chahng)* very
trolley   often

crowded. Let's learn how to take the **gōnggòngqìchē**, *(gohng-gohng-chee-chuh)* **dìtiě** *(dee-tee-eh)* **huòzhě diànchē**. *(dee-ahn-chuh)*
                                                                          subway   trolley

(dee-tee-eh)
dìtiě
subway

(gohng-gohng-chee-chuh)
gōnggòngqìchē
bus

(dee-tee-eh) (jahn)
dìtiě zhàn
subway   stop

(dee-ahn-chuh)
diànchē
trolley

(gohng-gohng-chee-chuh) (jahn)
gōnggòngqìchē zhàn
bus   stop

(dee-too)
Dìtú displaying the various **chē** *(chuh)* **zhàn** *(jahn)* **hé** **lù** *(loo)* are available at most major stops. Be sure to let
maps   stops   routes

the **shòupiàoyuán** *(shoh-pee-ow-yoo-ahn)* know where **nǐ** are going, because ticket prices are based on distances
conductor

traveled. This applies to both **gōnggòngqìchē** *(gohng-gohng-chee-chuh)* and **diànchē**. *(dee-ahn-chuh)*

❏	**Déguó** (duh-gwoh)	Germany	_____
❏	**Yīngguó** (yeeng-gwoh)	England	_____
❏	**Xībānyá** (ssee-bahn-yah)	Spain	_____
❏	**Fǎguó** (fah-gwoh)	France	_____
❏	**Yìdàlì** (yee-dah-lee)	Italy	_____

Other than having foreign words, the **dìtiě** *(dee-tee-eh)* functions just like the one in London **huòzhě** New York. Locate your destination, select the correct line on your practice **dìtiě** and hop on board.

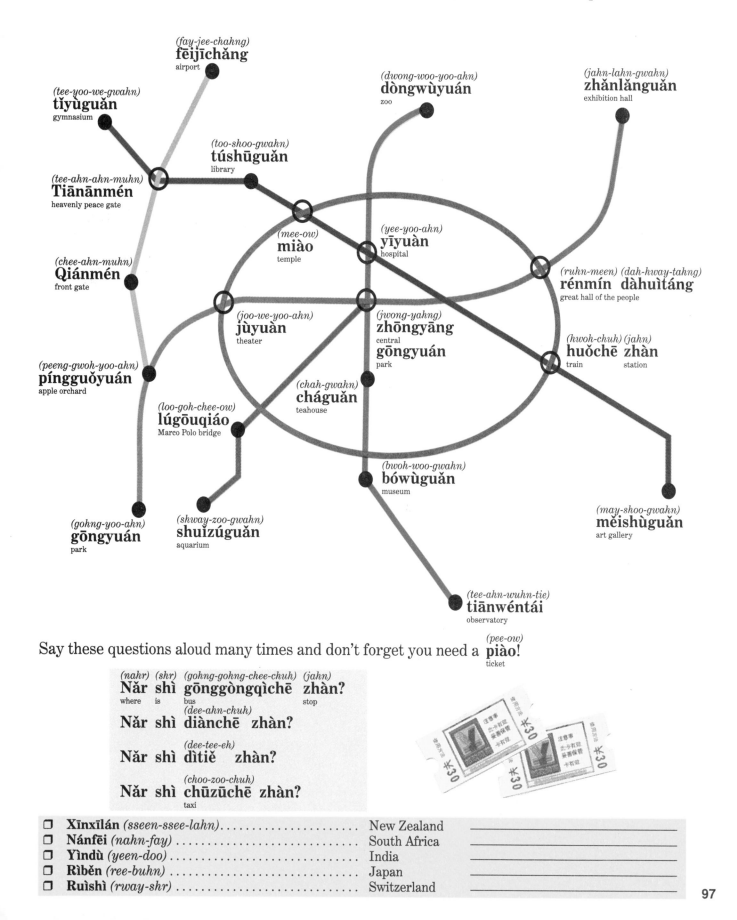

fēijīchǎng *(fay-jee-chahng)*
airport

tǐyùguǎn *(tee-yoo-we-gwahn)*
gymnasium

dòngwùyuán *(dwong-woo-yoo-ahn)*
zoo

zhǎnlǎnguǎn *(jahn-lahn-gwahn)*
exhibition hall

túshūguǎn *(too-shoo-gwahn)*
library

Tiānānmén *(tee-ahn-ahn-muhn)*
heavenly peace gate

miào *(mee-ow)*
temple

yīyuàn *(yee-yoo-ahn)*
hospital

Qiánmén *(chee-ahn-muhn)*
front gate

rénmín dàhuìtáng *(ruhn-meen) (dah-hway-tahng)*
great hall of the people

jùyuàn *(joo-we-yoo-ahn)*
theater

zhōngyāng gōngyuán *(jwong-yahng)*
central park

huǒchē zhàn *(hwoh-chuh) (jahn)*
train station

píngguǒyuán *(peeng-gwoh-yoo-ahn)*
apple orchard

lúgōuqiáo *(loo-goh-chee-ow)*
Marco Polo bridge

cháguǎn *(chah-gwahn)*
teahouse

bówùguǎn *(bwoh-woo-gwahn)*
museum

měishùguǎn *(may-shoo-gwahn)*
art gallery

gōngyuán *(gohng-yoo-ahn)*
park

shuǐzúguǎn *(shway-zoo-gwahn)*
aquarium

tiānwéntái *(tee-ahn-wuhn-tie)*
observatory

Say these questions aloud many times and don't forget you need a **piào**! *(pee-ow)*
ticket

Nǎr shì gōnggòngqìchē zhàn? *(nahr) (shr) (gohng-gohng-chee-chuh) (jahn)*
where is bus stop

Nǎr shì diànchē zhàn? *(dee-ahn-chuh)*

Nǎr shì dìtiě zhàn? *(dee-tee-eh)*

Nǎr shì chūzūchē zhàn? *(choo-zoo-chuh)*
taxi

☐ **Xīnxīlán** *(sseen-ssee-lahn)* . . . . New Zealand _____
☐ **Nánfēi** *(nahn-fay)* . . . . South Africa _____
☐ **Yìndù** *(yeen-doo)* . . . . India _____
☐ **Rìběn** *(ree-buhn)* . . . . Japan _____
☐ **Ruìshì** *(rway-shr)* . . . . Switzerland _____

Practice the following basic **wèntí** *(questions)* out loud and then **xiě** *(ssee-eh)* *(write)* them in the blanks **zài yòubiān.** *(yoh-bee-ahn)* *(right side)*

1. **Gōnggòngqìchē shénme** *(shun-muh)* *(what)* **shíhou** *(shr-hoh)* *(time/when)* **dào?** *(dow)* *(arrives)* _____

    Diànchē shénme shíhou dào? _____

    (dee-tee-eh)
    Dìxiàtiě shénme shíhou dào? _____

2. **Gōnggòngqìchē shénme shíhou kāi?** *(ki)* *(leaves)* _____

    Diànchē shénme shíhou kāi? _____

    (dee-tee-eh)
    Dìxiàtiě shénme shíhou kāi? _____

3. **Gōnggòngqìchē dào bówùguǎn duōshao** *(dwoh-shao)* *(how much)* **qián?** *(chee-ahn)* *(money)* _____

    Diànchē dào dòngwùyuán *(dwong-woo-yoo-ahn)* *(zoo)* **duōshao qián?** _____

    Dìxiàtiě dào lǚguǎn duōshao qián? _____

4. **Gōnggòngqìchē zhàn** *(jahn)* *(stop)* **zài** *(zi)* *(is)* **nǎr?** *(where)* _____

    Diànchē zhàn zài nǎr? _____

    (dee-tee-eh)
    Dìxiàtiě zhàn zài nǎr? _____

Let's change directions and learn these **xīn dòngcí.** **Nǐ** know the basic "plug-in" formula, so write out your own sentences using these new verbs.

(ssee)
xǐ _____
to wash

(dee-oo)
diū _____
to lose

(yow)
yào _____
to take (time)

Zhèr shì a few holidays which you might experience during your visit.
- ❐ **chūnjié** *(choon-jee-eh)* .... Chinese New Year
- ❐ **wǔyī láodòng jié** *(woo-yee)(lao-dohng)(jee-eh)* .... Labor Day (May 1)
- ❐ **guóqìng jié** *(gwoh-cheeng)(jee-eh)* .... National Day (October 1)
- ❐ **liùyī értóng jié** *(lee-oo-yee)(ur-tohng)(jee-eh)* .... Children's Day (June 1)

(my) Mǎi hé Mài
to buy   to sell

Zài wàiguó, *(why-gwoh)* shopping is **hěn** *(huhn)* **yǒuyìsi.** *(yoh-yee-suh)* The simple everyday task of buying **yì** *(my)* **píng** *(peeng)* **niúnǎi** *(nee-oo-ni)*
foreign country   very   interesting   bottle   milk

huòzhě yí ge píngguǒ *(peeng-gwoh)* becomes a challenge that **nǐ xiànzài** should be able to meet easily. Of
apple

course, **nǐ** will **mǎi** *(my)* **jìniànpǐn,** *(jee-nee-ahn-peen)* **yóupiào hé** *(yoh-pee-ow)* **míngxìnpiàn,** *(meeng-sseen-pee-ahn)* but do not forget those many other
buy   souvenirs   stamps

dōngxi *(dwong-ssee)* ranging from shoelaces to **āsīpīlín** *(ah-sih-pee-leen)* that **nǐ** might need unexpectedly. Locate your
things   aspirin

store, draw a line to it and, as always, write your new words in the blanks provided.

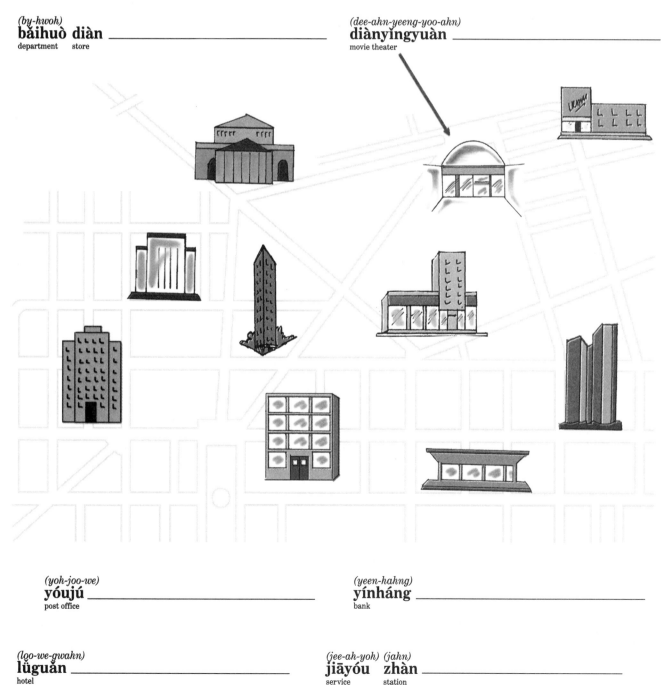

(by-hwoh)
bǎihuò diàn _____
department   store

(dee-ahn-yeeng-yoo-ahn)
diànyǐngyuàn _____
movie theater

(yoh-joo-we)
yóujú _____
post office

(yeen-hahng)
yínháng _____
bank

(loo-we-gwahn)
lǚguǎn _____
hotel

(jee-ah-yoh) *(jahn)*
jiāyóu zhàn _____
service   station

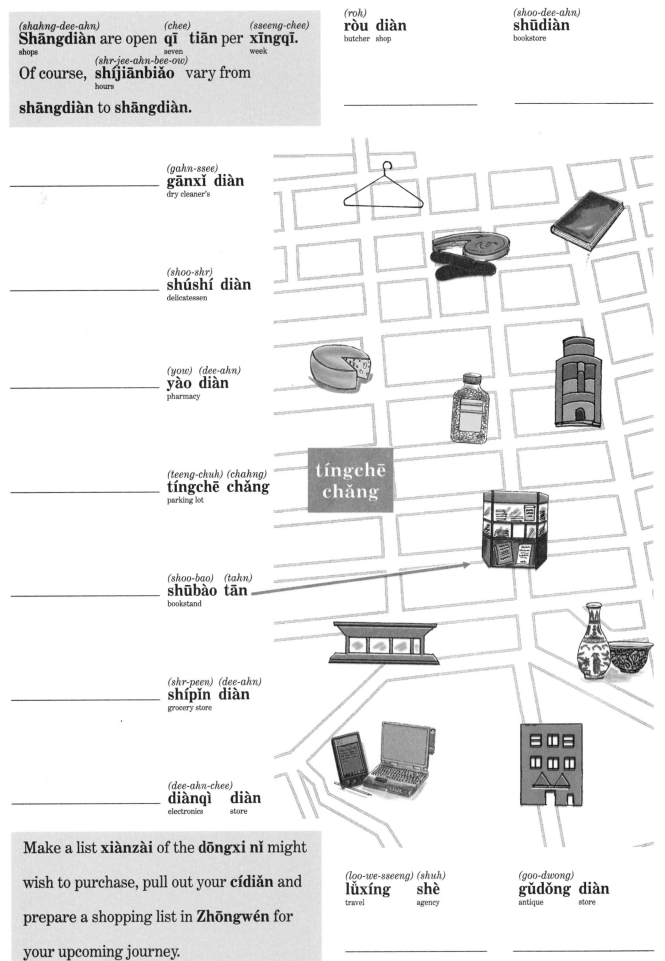

(shahng-dee-ahn)
Shāngdiàn are open **qī** **tiān** per **xīngqī.**
shops   *(chee)* seven   *(sseng-chee)* week

(shr-jee-ahn-bee-ow)
Of course, **shíjiānbiǎo** vary from
hours

shāngdiàn to **shāngdiàn.**

(roh)
ròu diàn
butcher shop

(shoo-dee-ahn)
shūdiàn
bookstore

_____   _____

(gahn-ssee)
_____ **gānxǐ diàn**
dry cleaner's

(shoo-shr)
_____ **shúshí diàn**
delicatessen

(yow) (dee-ahn)
_____ **yào diàn**
pharmacy

(teeng-chuh) (chahng)
_____ **tíngchē chǎng**
parking lot

tíngchē chǎng

(shoo-bao) (tahn)
_____ **shūbào tān**
bookstand

(shr-peen) (dee-ahn)
_____ **shípǐn diàn**
grocery store

(dee-ahn-chee)
_____ **diànqì diàn**
electronics   store

Make a list **xiànzài** of the **dōngxi nǐ** might

wish to purchase, pull out your **cídiǎn** and

prepare a shopping list in **Zhōngwén** for

your upcoming journey.

(loo-we-sseeng) (shuh)
lǚxíng shè
travel   agency

(goo-dwong)
gǔdǒng diàn
antique   store

_____   _____

(nee-oo-ni) (dee-ahn)
niúnǎi diàn
dairy

(hwahr)
huār diàn
flower shop

(yoo-we) (dee-ahn)
yú diàn _____
fish shop

_____   _____

(shway-gwoh)
shuǐguǒ diàn _____
fruit

(tsi-chahng)
càichǎng *càichǎng, càichǎng*
market

(jee-nee-ahn-peen)
jìniànpǐn diàn _____
souvenir

(jwong-bee-ow)
zhōngbiǎo diàn _____
watchmaker's

(mee-ahn-bao) (dee-ahn)
miànbāo diàn _____
bakery

(kah-fay)
kāfēi diàn _____
coffee shop

(ssee-yee)
xǐyī diàn _____
laundry

(wuhn-joo-we)
wénjù diàn
stationery store

(lee-fah)
lǐfà diàn
hairdresser's

_____   _____

ground (first) floor =	yī *(loh)* lóu
second floor =	*(ur)* èr lóu
third floor =	sān lóu

101

(by-hwoh) *(dee-ahn)*
Bǎihuò Diàn
department   store

At this point, **nǐ** should just about be ready for **nǐde Zhōngguó lǚxíng.** *(nee-duh)* *(loo-we-sseeng)* **Nǐ** have gone

shopping for those last-minute odds 'n ends. Most likely, the store directory at your local

(by-hwoh)
bǎihuò diàn did not look like the one **xiàbiān! Nǐ zhīdào** that **"nǔrén"** *(noo-we-ruhn)* **shì Zhōngwén** for
department   store   know

"women" so if **nǐ xūyào** *(ssee-oo-yow)* something for a **nǔren, nǐ** would probably look on which floor?
need

5	楼	yínqì	银器	(silver)
		diànqì	电器	(electronics)
		bōlí	玻璃	(glassware)
		shíwù	食物	(food)
4	楼	shū	书籍	(books)
		wénjù	文具	(stationery)
		wánjù	玩具	(toys)
		jiājù	家俱	(furniture)
3	楼	nánzhuāng	男装	(men's clothing)
		nǔzhuāng	女装	(women's clothing)
		gùkè fúwù	顾客服务台	(customer service)
2	楼	xié	鞋	(shoes)
		gōngjù	工具	(tools)
		yùndòng yòngpǐn	运动用品	(sporting goods)
1	楼	zhàoxiàng yòngpǐn	照相用品	(cameras)
		zhūbǎo	珠宝	(jewelry)
		pízhì pǐn	皮制品	(leather)
		zhōngbiǎo	钟表	(clocks & watches)

Let's start a checklist for **nǐde lǚxíng.** Besides **yīfu,** *(yee-foo)* **nǐ hái** *(hi)* **xūyào** *(ssee-oo-yow)* to buy **shénme?** *(shun-muh)* As
clothes   still   need   what

you learn these **cí** assemble these items **zài qiángjiǎo** *(chee-ahng-jee-ow)* of your **fángzi.** Check and make sure
corner

that they are clean and ready for **nǐde lǚxíng.** On the next pages, match each item to its picture,

draw a line to it and write out the word many times. As **nǐ** organize these things, check them off

on this list. Do not forget to take the next group of sticky labels and label these **dōngxi** today.

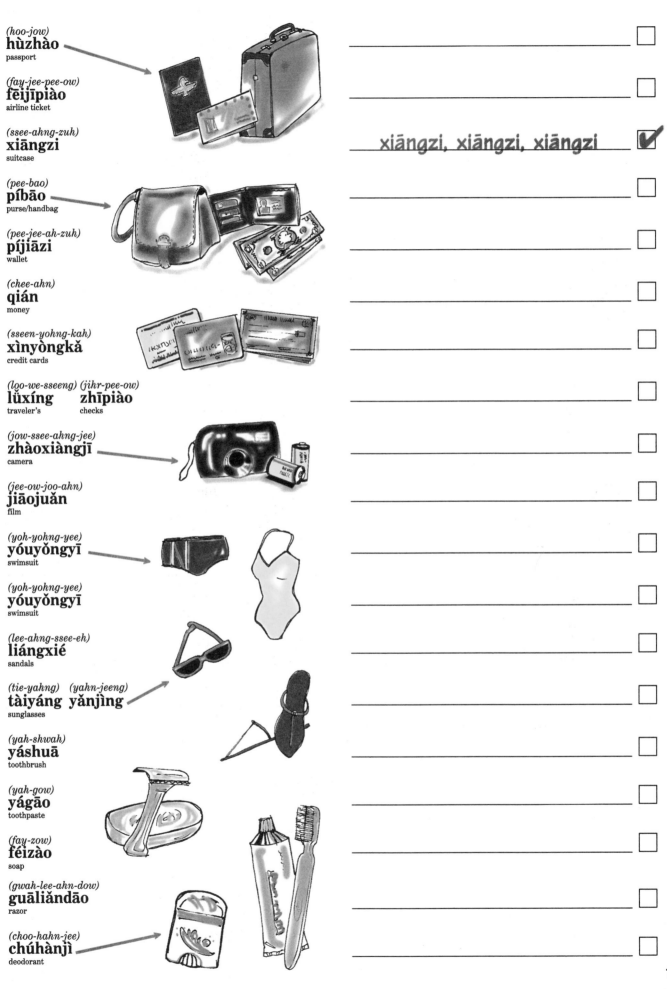

(hoo-jow)
hùzhào
passport

(fay-jee-pee-ow)
fēijīpiào
airline ticket

(ssee-ahng-zuh)
xiāngzi
suitcase

__xiāngzi, xiāngzi, xiāngzi__ ☑

(pee-bao)
píbāo
purse/handbag

(pee-jee-ah-zuh)
píjiāzi
wallet

(chee-ahn)
qián
money

(sseen-yohng-kah)
xìnyòngkǎ
credit cards

(loo-we-sseeng) (jihr-pee-ow)
lǚxíng zhīpiào
traveler's   checks

(jow-ssee-ahng-jee)
zhàoxiàngjī
camera

(jee-ow-joo-ahn)
jiāojuǎn
film

(yoh-yohng-yee)
yóuyǒngyī
swimsuit

(yoh-yohng-yee)
yóuyǒngyī
swimsuit

(lee-ahng-ssee-eh)
liángxié
sandals

(tie-yahng) (yahn-jeeng)
tàiyáng yǎnjìng
sunglasses

(yah-shwah)
yáshuā
toothbrush

(yah-gow)
yágāo
toothpaste

(fay-zow)
féizào
soap

(gwah-lee-ahn-dow)
guāliǎndāo
razor

(choo-hahn-jee)
chúhànjì
deodorant

103

(shoo-zuh)
shūzi
comb

shūzi, shūzi, shūzi, shūzi ✓

(yoo-we-yee)
yǔyī
raincoat

(sahn)
sǎn
umbrella

(dah-yee)
dàyī
overcoat

(shoh-tao)
shǒutào
gloves

(mao-zuh)
màozi
hat

(mao-zuh)
màozi
hat

(ssee-yoo-eh-zuh)
xuēzi
boots

(ssee-eh)
xié
shoes

(yoon-dohng-ssee-eh)
yùndòngxié
tennis shoes

(ssee-jwahng)
xīzhuāng
suit

(leeng-die)
lǐngdài
tie

(chuhn-yee)
chènyī
shirt

(shoh-joo-ahn)
shǒujuàn
handkerchief

(why-tao)
wàitào
jacket

(koo-zuh)
kùzi
trousers

(nee-oo-zi-koo)
niúzǎikù
jeans

(dwahn-koo)
duǎnkù
shorts

(wuhn-hwah-shahn)
wénhuàshán
T-shirt

(nay-koo)
nèikù
underpants

(nay-yee)
nèiyī
undershirt

(lee-ahn-yee-choon)
liányīqún
dress

(chuhn-yee)
chènyī
blouse

(choon-zuh)
qúnzi
skirt

qúnzi, qúnzi, qúnzi, qúnzi ✔

(mao-yee)
máoyī
sweater

(chuhn-choon)
chènqún
slip

(ssee-wong-jow)
xiōngzhào
bra

(nay-koo)
nèikù
underpants

(wah-zuh)
wàzi
socks

(koo-wah)
kùwà
pantyhose

(shway-yee)
shuìyī
pajamas

(shway-yee)
shuìyī
nightshirt

(shway-pow)
shuìpáo
bathrobe

(twoh-ssee-eh)
tuōxié
slippers

From now on, **nǐ** *(yoh)* **yǒu** " *(fay-zow)* **féizào**" and not "soap." Having assembled these **dōngxi, nǐ** are ready
have   things

for **nǐde lǚxíng.** Let's add these important shopping phrases to your basic repertoire.
your

Shénme *(chee-tsoon)* **chǐcùn?** _____
what   measurement

(shr-huh)
Shìhé. _____
it fits

(boo) (shr-huh)
Bú shìhé. _____
it does not fit

Treat yourself to a final review. **Nǐ** know the **míngzì** for **Zhōngguó** **shāngdiàn** *(shahng-dee-ahn)*, so let's practice

shopping. Just remember your key question **cí** that you learned in Step 2. Whether **nǐ** need to

buy a **màozi** *(mao-zuh)* **huòzhě** a **shū** the necessary **cí** are the same.
or

names

1.   First step — **nǎr?**

Yào diàn zài nǎr? *(yow) (dee-ahn)*
pharmacy

Yínháng zài nǎr?
bank

Diànyǐngyuàn zài nǎr? *(dee-ahn-yeeng-yoo-ahn)*
movie theater

Bǎihuò diàn zài nǎr? *(by-hwoh)*
department

_____

(Where is the bakery?)

_____

(Where is the grocery store?)

_____

(Where is the market?)

2.   Second step — tell them what **nǐ** **xūyào** *(ssee-oo-yow)* **huòzhě** **xiǎng** *(ssee-ahng)* **yào!** *(yow)*
need   would like

Wǒ xūyào . . . *(ssee-oo-yow)*
I   need

Wǒ xiǎng yào . . .
I   would like

Nǐmen yǒu . . . ma? *(yoh)*
do you have

_____

(Do you have postcards?)

_____

(I would like four stamps.)

_____

(I need toothpaste.)

_____

(I need film.)

_____

(Do you have coffee?)

Go through the glossary at the end of this **shū** and select **èrshí ge cí**. *(ur-shr)* Drill the above patterns with **zhè èrshí ge cí**. Don't cheat. Drill them **jīntiān**. *(jeen-tee-ahn)* **Xiànzài**, take **èrshí ge cí** more from *twenty*

(nee-duh) (tsih-dee-ahn)
nǐde cídiǎn and do the same.
your   dictionary

3. Third step — find out **duōshao qián.** *(dwoh-shao)* *(chee-ahn)*
                                          how much   money

(nah)
Nà ge duōshao?   **Nà ge duōshao qián?**   **Qiānbǐ duōshao qián?** *(chee-ahn-bee)*
that   pencil

_____
(How much does the toothpaste cost?)

_____
(How much does the soap cost?)

_____
(How much does a cup of tea cost?)

4.   Fourth step — success! I found it!

(jihr-dow)   *(shwoh)*
Once **nǐ zhīdào** what **nǐ** would like, **nǐ shuō**,
                                                    say

(juh)
Wǒ xiǎng yào zhè ge. _____
                  this

or simply,

(yow)
Wǒ yào. _____
      want

Huòzhě, if **nǐ** don't want something, **nǐ shuō**,

(boo) (ssee-hoo-ahn)
Wǒ bù xǐhuān nà ge. _____
      don't like

or

Wǒ bù yào. _____

Congratulations! You have finished. By now you should have stuck your labels, flashed your cards, cut out your menu guide and packed your suitcases. You should be very pleased with your accomplishment. You have learned what it sometimes takes others years to achieve and you

hopefully had fun doing it. **Yí lù píng ān!** *(ahn)*
                           safe and peaceful journey

Glossary

This glossary contains words used in this book only. It is not meant to be a dictionary. Consider purchasing a dictionary which best suits your needs - small for traveling, large for reference, or specialized for specific vocabulary needs.

A

ǎi *(I)* .... short
Āodàlìyá *(ow-dah-lee-yah)* .... Australia
Āodìlì *(ow-dee-lee)* .... Austria
āsīpīlín *(ah-sih-pee-leen)* .... aspirin

B

bā *(bah)* .... eight, scar
bá *(bah)* .... to pull up
bǎ *(bah)* .... measure word (M)
bà *(bah)* .... father
bābǎi *(bah-by)* .... eight hundred
bái *(by)* .... white
bǎi *(by)* .... (hundred) combined with other numbers
báicài *(by-tsi)* .... cabbage
bǎihuò diàn *(by-hwoh)(dee-ahn)* ... department store
bàn *(bahn)* .... half, half past
bàngōngshì *(bahn-gohng-shr)* .... office
bāoguǒ *(bao-gwoh)* .... parcel
bǎoshí *(bao-shr)* .... gem
bàozhǐ *(bao-jihr)* .... newspaper
bāshí *(bah-shr)* .... eighty
bāyuè *(bah-yoo-eh)* .... August
bēi *(bay)* .... glass, cup (M)
běi *(bay)* .... north
běibiān *(bay-bee-ahn)* .... North
běifāng *(bay-fahng)* .... northern
bēizi *(bay-zuh)* .... cup, mug
bèizi *(bay-zuh)* .... quilt
běn *(buhn)* .... bound together (M)
běndì cháhàotái *(buhn-dee)(chah-how-tie)* ....
.... local directory assistance
běndì diànhuà *(buhn-dee)(dee-ahn-hwah)* ... local telephone call
bǐ *(bee)* .... pen, writing instrument
biān *(bee-ahn)* .... side
biǎogé *(bee-ow-guh)* .... form, schedule
bǐjī *(bee-jee)* .... handwriting
bǐjì *(bee-jee)* .... to take notes
bǐjìběn *(bee-jee-buhn)* .... notebook
Bǐlìshí *(bee-lee-shr)* .... Belgium
bīng *(beeng)* .... ice
bìng *(beeng)* .... sick
bīngbáo *(beeng-bao)* .... hail
bīnggùn *(beeng-goon)* .... popsicle
bīngkuài *(beeng-kwhy)* .... ice cubes
bīngqílín *(beeng-chee-leen)* .... ice cream
bīngshān *(beeng-shahn)* .... iceberg
bīngshuāng *(beeng-shwahng)* .... frost
bīngtáng *(beeng-tahng)* .... rock candy
bīnguǎn *(been-gwahn)* ... hotel for foreign tourists
bīngxiāng *(beeng-ssee-ahng)* .... refrigerator
bīngxié *(beeng-ssee-eh)* .... ice skates
bīngzhù *(beeng-joo)* .... icicle
bǐxīn *(bee-sseen)* .... pen/pencil refill
bōcài *(bwoh-tsi)* .... spinach
bōlí *(bwoh-lee)* .... glassware
bōlíbēi *(bwoh-lee-bay)* .... glass
108 **bówùguǎn** *(bwoh-woo-gwahn)* .... museum

bù, bú *(boo)* .... no, not
bù hǎo *(boo)(how)* .... not good, bad
bù néng jìnqù *(boo)(nung)(jeen-chee-oo)* ...... do not enter
bú shìhé *(boo)(shr-huh)* .... it does not fit
bú xiè *(boo)(ssee-eh)* .... you're welcome
bú yào *(boo)(yow)* .... don't want it
búshìhé *(boo-shr-huh)* .... it does not fit
bùxié *(boo-ssee-eh)* .... cotton shoes

C

cài *(tsi)* .... vegetables, food dishes
càichǎng *(tsi-chahng)* .... market
càidān *(tsi-dahn)* .... menu
càidiàn *(tsi-dee-ahn)* .... vegetable store
càihuā *(tsi-hwah)* .... cauliflower
càiyuán *(tsi-yoo-ahn)* .... vegetable garden
càiyóu *(tsi-yoh)* .... vegetable oil
càizǐr *(tsi-zur)* .... vegetable seeds
cānchē *(tsahn-chuh)* .... dining car
cānjīn *(tsahn-jeen)* .... napkin
cǎo *(tsow)* .... grass
cèsuǒ *(tsuh-swoh)* .... lavatory
chá *(chah)* .... tea
chábēi *(chah-bay)* .... tea cup
chàbùduō *(chah-boo-dwoh)* .... about
chádiǎn *(chah-dee-ahn)* .... light meal
cháguǎn *(chah-gwahn)* .... teahouse
cháhuā *(chah-hwah)* .... camelia
cháhuì *(chah-hway)* .... tea party
chájī *(chah-jee)* .... coffee table
chájù *(chah-joo)* .... tea service
cháng *(chahng)* .... long
chángcháng *(chahng-chahng)* ...... often, generally
Chángchéng *(chahng-chuhng)* .... the Great Wall
chángtú cháhàotái *(chahng-too)(chah-how-tie)* ....
.... long-distance directory assistance
chángtú diànhuà *(chahng-too)(dee-ahn-hwah)* ....
.... long-distance telephone call
chángyǐ *(chahng-yee)* .... bench
chāntīng *(chahn-teeng)* .... hotel café
chǎo *(chow)* .... stir-fried
cháshuǐ *(chah-shway)* .... drink (tea, etc.)
cháyè *(chah-yeh)* .... tea leaf
chāzi *(chah-zuh)* .... fork
chē *(chuh)* .... vehicle, car, cart
chēkù *(chuh-koo)* .... garage
chènqún *(chuhn-choon)* .... underslip
chènyī *(chuhn-yee)* .... shirt, blouse
chēpái *(chuh-pie)* .... license plate
chēxiāng *(chuh-ssee-ahng)* .... compartment
chēzhàn *(chuh-jahn)* .... bus/vehicle stop
chī *(chr)* .... to eat, eats, eat
chǐcùn *(chee-tsoon)* .... measurement, size
chīfàn *(chr-fahn)* .... let's eat, to eat a meal
chuán *(chwahn)* .... boat
chuáng *(chwahng)* .... bed
chuānghù *(chwahng-hoo)* .... window
chuánzhēn *(chwahn-juhn)* .... fax
chúfáng *(choo-fahng)* .... kitchen

chúhànjì (*choo-hahn-jee*) . . . . deodorant
chūkǒu (*choo-koh*) . . . . exit
chūnjié (*choon-jee-eh*) . . . . Chinese New Year
chūnjuǎn (*choon-joo-ahn*) . . . . spring roll
chūntiān (*choon-tee-ahn*) . . . . spring
chūzūchē (*choo-zoo-chuh*) . . . . taxi
cí (*tsih*) . . . . word
cídiǎn (*tsih-dee-ahn*) . . . . dictionary
cóng (*tswong*) . . . . from

D

dǎ (*dah*) . . . . to make (telephone call, telegram)
dà (*dah*) . . . . big, size
dàdào (*dah-dow*) . . . . boulevard
dài (*die*) . . . . to bring
dài (*die*) . . . . with
dàn (*dahn*) . . . . egg
dānchéng (*dahn-chuhng*) . . . . one-way
Dānmài (*dahn-my*) . . . . Denmark
dānrénfáng (*dahn-ruhn-fahng*) . . . . single room
dào (*dow*) . . . . to, to arrive, arrival
dāozi (*dow-zuh*) . . . . knife
dàyī (*dah-yee*) . . . . overcoat
de (*duh*) . . . . added to word when an adjective
Déguó (*duh-gwoh*) . . . . Germany
dēng (*dung*) . . . . lamp, light
děng (*dung*) . . . . class of travel
děng (*dung*) . . . . to wait, waits, wait
Déwén (*duh-wuhn*) . . . . German
dī (*dee*) . . . . low
diǎn (*dee-ahn*) . . . . o'clock
diàn (*dee-ahn*) . . . . store, shop
diàn (*dee-ahn*) . . . . electricity
diànbào (*dee-ahn-bao*) . . . . telegram
diànchē (*dee-ahn-chuh*) . . . . trolley
diànchē zhàn (*dee-ahn-chuh*)(*jahn*) . . . . trolley stop
diànchí (*dee-ahn-chee*) . . . . battery
diànhuà (*dee-ahn-hwah*) . . . . . . telephone, telephone call
diànhuà bù (*dee-ahn-hwah*)(*boo*) . . . telephone book/register
diànhuà kǎ (*dee-ahn-hwah*)(*kah*) . . . . telephone card
diànhuà tíng (*dee-ahn-hwah*)(*teeng*) . . . . . . telephone booth
diànnǎo (*dee-ahn-now*) . . . . computer
diànqì (*dee-ahn-chee*) . . . . electronics
diànqì diàn (*dee-ahn-chee*)(*dee-ahn*) . . . . . electronics store
diànshì (*dee-ahn-shr*) . . . . television
diàntái (*dee-ahn-tie*) . . . . radio station
diàntī (*dee-ahn-tee*) . . . . elevator
diàntǒng (*dee-ahn-twong*) . . . . flashlight
diǎnxīn (*dee-ahn-sseen*) . . . . snack
diǎnxíngde (*dee-ahn-sseeng-duh*) . . . . typical
diànyǐng (*dee-ahn-yeeng*) . . . . movie
diànyǐngyuàn (*dee-ahn-yeeng-yoo-ahn*) . . . . movie theater
diànyuán (*dee-ahn-yoo-ahn*) . . . . store clerk
diànzhǔ (*dee-ahn-joo*) . . . . storekeeper
diāokè (*dee-ow-kuh*) . . . . carvings
dìbā (*dee-bah*) . . . . eighth
dìbǎn (*dee-bahn*) . . . . floor
dìfāng (*dee-fahng*) . . . . place
dìng (*deeng*) . . . . to book, reserve
dìngdān (*deeng-dahn*) . . . . order form
dìqī (*dee-chee*) . . . . seventh
dìtú (*dee-too*) . . . . map
diū (*dee-oo*) . . . . to lose
dìxiàshì (*dee-ssee-ah-shr*) . . . . basement
dìtiě (*dee-tee-eh*) . . . . subway
dìtiě zhàn (*dee-tee-eh*)(*jahn*) . . . . subway stop
dōng (*dwong*) . . . . east

dǒng (*dwong*) . . . . . to understand, understands, understand
dōngbiān (*dwong-bee-ahn*) . . . . East
dòngcí (*dwong-tsih*) . . . . verb
dōngfāng (*dwong-fahng*) . . . . eastern, oriental
dōngnán (*dwong-nahn*) . . . . east-south
dōngtiān (*dwong-tee-ahn*) . . . . winter
dòngwùyuán (*dwong-woo-yoo-ahn*) . . . . zoo
dōngxi (*dwong-ssee*) . . . . thing
dōu (*doh*) . . . . all
dòu (*doh*) . . . . bean
dòufu (*doh-foo*) . . . . bean curd
dòushā (*doh-shah*) . . . . bean paste
dòuyá (*doh-yah*) . . . . bean sprouts
dòuyóu (*doh-yoh*) . . . . soybean oil
dù (*doo*) . . . . degrees
duǎn (*dwahn*) . . . . short
duǎnkù (*dwahn-koo*) . . . . shorts
duìbùqǐ (*dway-boo-chee*) . . . . . . I'm sorry, excuse me
duìhuà (*dway-hwah*) . . . . conversation
duìhuàn chù (*dway-hwahn*)(*choo*) . . . money-exchange office
duō (*dwoh*) . . . . many, much, more, a lot
duōshao (*dwoh-shao*) . . . . how much, how many
duōshao qián (*dwoh-shao*)(*chee-ahn*) . . . .
. . . . how much does that cost, how much money

E

é (*uh*) . . . . goose
èr (*ur*) . . . . two, second
èrbǎi (*ur-by*) . . . . two hundred
èrshí (*ur-shr*) . . . . twenty
èryuè (*ur-yoo-eh*) . . . . February
érzi (*ur-zuh*) . . . . son

F

Fǎguó (*fah-gwoh*) . . . . France
fàn (*fahn*) . . . . meal, rice
fàndiàn (*fahn-dee-ahn*) . . . . tourist hotel
fāng (*fahng*) . . . . direction
fáng (*fahng*) . . . . room, apartment
fángdōng (*fahng-dwong*) . . . . landlord
fāngfǎ (*fahng-fah*) . . . . ways
fángjiān (*fahng-jee-ahn*) . . . . room
fángkè (*fahng-kuh*) . . . . tenant
fànguǎn (*fahn-gwahn*) . . . . restaurant
fángzi (*fahng-zuh*) . . . . house
fángzide (*fahng-zuh-duh*) . . . . house's
fàntīng (*fahn-teeng*) . . . . dining room
Fǎwén (*fah-wuhn*) . . . . French
fēi (*fay*) . . . . to fly, flies, fly
fēijī (*fay-jee*) . . . . airplane
fēijīchǎng (*fay-jee-chahng*) . . . . airport
fēijīkù (*fay-jee-koo*) . . . . hangar (airport)
fēijīpiào (*fay-jee-pee-ow*) . . . . airplane ticket
fēiqín (*fay-cheen*) . . . . birds
fēisù (*fay-soo*) . . . . quickly
fēiwǔ (*fay-woo*) . . . . to flutter
fēixíng (*fay-sseeng*) . . . . to soar
fēixíngyuán (*fay-sseeng-yoo-ahn*) . . . . pilot
fēiyú (*fay-yoo-we*) . . . . flying fish
féizào (*fay-zow*) . . . . soap
fēn (*fuhn*) . . . . minute, unit of Chinese money
fěnbǐ (*fuhn-bee*) . . . . chalk
fēng (*fung*) . . . . measure word (M)
fēngqín (*fung-cheen*) . . . . organ
fěnhóng (*fuhn-hohng*) . . . . pink
fójiào (*fwoh-jee-ow*) . . . . Buddhist **109**

fù qián (foo)(chee-ahn) . . . . to pay, pay for
fùmǔ (foo-moo) . . . . parents
fùqin (foo-cheen) . . . . father
fúwùyuán (foo-woo-yoo-ahn) . . . . service person

G

gānbēi (gahn-bay) . . . . cheers!
gāngbǐ (gahng-bee) . . . . fountain pen
gāngqín (gahng-cheen) . . . . piano
gānxǐ diàn (gahn-ssee)(dee-ahn) . . . . dry cleaner's
gāo (gao) . . . . high, tall
ge (guh) . . . . measure word (M)
gēge (guh-guh) . . . . (older) brother
géi (gay) . . . . for
gěi (gay) . . . . to give, give, gives
gěi wǒ (gay)(woh) . . . . give me
gēzi (guh-zuh) . . . . pigeon
gōnggòngqìchē (gohng-gohng-chee-chuh) . . . . bus
gōnggòngqìchē zhàn (gohng-gohng-chee-chuh)(jahn) . . . . . .
. . . . bus stop
gōngjù (gohng-joo-we) . . . . tools
gōngyìpǐn (gohng-yee-peen) . . . . artworks
gōngyòng diànhuà (gohng-yohng)(dee-ahn-hwah) . . . .
. . . . public telephone
gōngyù (gohng-yoo-we) . . . . apartment, boarding room
gōngyuán (gohng-yoo-ahn) . . . . park
gǒu (goh) . . . . dog
guāfēng (gwah-fung) . . . . windy
guāliǎndāo (gwah-lee-ahn-dow) . . . . razor
guǎn (gwahn) . . . . place, hall
guānmén (gwahn-muhn) . . . . closed, closes
gǔdǒng diàn (goo-dwong)(dee-ahn) . . . . antique store
gūgu (goo-goo) . . . . aunt
guì (gway) . . . . expensive
guìtái (gway-tie) . . . . counter
guìzi (gway-zuh) . . . . cupboard
gùkè fúwù (goo-kuh)(foo-woo) . . . . customer service
guó (gwoh) . . . . country, nation, state
guógē (gwoh-guh) . . . . national anthem
guóhuì (gwoh-hway) . . . . parliament
guójí (gwoh-jee) . . . . nationality
guójiā (gwoh-jee-ah) . . . . country
guómín (gwoh-meen) . . . . people of a country
guónèi (gwoh-nay) . . . . domestic
guóqí (gwoh-chee) . . . . national flag
guóqìng jié (gwoh-cheeng)(jee-eh) . . National Day (October 1)
guówài (gwoh-why) . . . . international
guówáng (gwoh-wahng) . . . . king
guóyíng (gwoh-yeeng) . . . . state-owned

H

hái (hi) . . . . still
hǎi (hi) . . . . sea
hǎi àn (hi)(ahn) . . . . coast
hǎi lán bǎoshí (hi)(lahn)(bao-shr) . . . . aquamarine
hǎigǎng (hi-gahng) . . . . seaport, harbor
hǎiguān (hi-gwahn) . . . . customs
hǎimián (hi-mee-ahn) . . . . sponge
háishì (hi-shr) . . . . or
hǎitān (hi-tahn) . . . . beach
hǎiwài (hi-why) . . . . overseas
hǎiwān (hi-wahn) . . . . bay, gulf
hǎiwèi (hi-way) . . . . seafood
hǎixiān (hi-ssee-ahn) . . . . seafood
hǎiyáng (hi-yahng) . . . . ocean
hángkōngxìn (hahng-kwong-sseen) . . . . airmail
110 hǎo (how) . . . . good, well, okay, all right

hào (how) . . . . number
hǎochī (how-chr) . . . . delicious
hǎochù (how-choo) . . . . benefit
hǎogǎn (how-gahn) . . . . good impression
hǎohàn (how-hahn) . . . . wise man, hero
hǎokàn (how-kahn) . . . . good-looking
hǎotīng (how-teeng) . . . . pleasant to the ear
hǎoxiào (how-ssee-ow) . . . . funny
hǎoyì (how-yee) . . . . goodwill
hǎoyùn (how-yoon) . . . . good fortune
hē (huh) . . . . to drink, drinks, drink
hé (huh) . . . . and
hēi (hay) . . . . black
Hélán (huh-lahn) . . . . Netherlands
hěn (huhn) . . . . very
hóng (hohng) . . . . red
hóng bǎoshí (hohng)(bao-shr) . . . . ruby
hòubiān (hoh-bee-ahn) . . . . behind
hòuchēshì (hoh-chuh-shr) . . . . waiting room
huā (hwah) . . . . flower, multi-colored
huà (hwah) . . . . language
huā duǒ (hwah)(dwoh) . . . . blossom
huài (hwhy) . . . . bad
huàn chē (hwahn)(chuh) . . . . to transfer (vehicles)
huáng (hwahng) . . . . yellow
huā píng (hwah)(peeng) . . . . flower vase
huā quān (hwah)(chwahn) . . . . wreath
huā shù (hwah)(shoo) . . . . bouquet
huār (hwahr) . . . . flower
huār diàn (hwahr)(dee-ahn) . . . . flower shop
huàr (hwahr) . . . . picture
huáshì (hwah-shr) . . . . Fahrenheit
huāyuán (hwah-yoo-ahn) . . . . garden
huī (hway) . . . . gray
huíjiào (hway-jee-ow) . . . . Moslem
hújiāo (hoo-jee-ow) . . . . pepper
huǒ (hwoh) . . . . fire, flame
huǒchái (hwoh-chi) . . . . match
huǒchē (hwoh-chuh) . . . . train
huǒchē zhàn (hwoh-chuh)(jahn) . . . . train station
huǒchē zǒng zhàn (hwoh-chuh)(zwong)(jahn) . . . .
. . . . main train station
huǒjiàn (hwoh-jee-ahn) . . . . rocket
huǒshān (hwoh-shahn) . . . . volcano
huòzhě (hwoh-juh) . . . . or
hùzhào (hoo-jow) . . . . passport

J

jī (jee) . . . . chicken
jǐ (jee) . . . . some, several
jǐ (jee) . . . . how many
jì (jee) . . . . to send by mail, mail
jǐ diǎn le? (jee)(dee-ahn)(luh) . . . . what time is it?
jiā (jee-ah) . . . . home
jiāhuo (jee-ah-hwoh) . . . . . (that) thing, guy, weapon
jiājù (jee-ah-joo-we) . . . . furniture
jiān (jee-ahn) . . . . measure word (M)
Jiānádà (jee-ah-nah-dah) . . . . Canada
Jiānádà rén (jee-ah-nah-dah)(ruhn) . . . . Canadian
jiàngluò (jee-ahng-lwoh) . . . . to land
jiànkāng (jee-ahn-kahng) . . . . healthy
jiànkāng zhèngmíng shū (jee-ahn-kahng)(jung-meeng)
(shoo) . . . . health certificate
jiǎo (jee-ow) . . . . unit of Chinese money
jiào (jee-ow) . . . . to be called, named
jiào (jee-ow) . . . . to ask, yell, call for
jiào (jee-ow) . . . . to order, orders, order

jiāojuǎn *(jee-ow-joo-ahn)* . . . . film
jiàqián *(jee-ah-chee-ahn)* . . . . prices
jiārén *(jee-ah-ruhn)* . . . . family members
jiātíng *(jee-ah-teeng)* . . . . family
jiāyóu zhàn *(jee-ah-yoh)(jahn)* . . . . service station
jīdàn *(jee-dahn)* . . . . chicken eggs
jīdūjiào *(jee-doo-jee-ow)* . . . . Protestant
jiē *(jee-eh)* . . . . street
jié *(jee-eh)* . . . . to clear, pay, close
jiézhàng *(jee-eh-jahng)* . . . . to pay a bill
jīn *(jeen)* . . . . golden
jìn *(jeen)* . . . . into, in
jīn nián *(jeen)(nee-ahn)* . . . . this year
jìn zhǐ tōng xíng *(jeen)(jihr)(twong)(sseng)* . . no trespassing
jìn zhǐ zhàoxiàng *(jeen)(jihr)(jow-ssee-ahng)* . . . .
. . . . no photos allowed
jǐngchá *(jeeng-chah)* . . . . police
jīnglǐ *(jeeng-lee)* . . . . manager
jìngzi *(jeeng-zuh)* . . . . mirror
jìniànpǐn *(jee-nee-ahn-peen)* . . . . souvenirs
jìniànpǐn diàn *(jee-nee-ahn-peen)(dee-ahn)* . . souvenir store
jīntiān *(jeen-tee-ahn)* . . . . today
jīpiào *(jee-pee-ow)* . . . . flight
jípǔchē *(jee-poo-chuh)* . . . . jeep
jiǔ *(jee-oo)* . . . . wine
jiǔ *(jee-oo)* . . . . nine
jiǔ guǎn *(jee-oo)(gwahn)* . . . . tavern
jiǔbǎi *(jee-oo-by)* . . . . nine hundred
jiǔbēi *(jee-oo-bay)* . . . . wine glass
jiǔdiàn *(jee-oo-dee-ahn)* . . . . hotel for foreign tourists
jiùmìng *(jee-oo-meeng)* . . . . help!
jiǔshí *(jee-oo-shr)* . . . . ninety
jiǔyuè *(jee-oo-yoo-eh)* . . . . September
jīyā *(jee-yah)* . . . . poultry
júhóngsè *(joo-hohng-suh)* . . . . orange
júhuā *(joo-hwah)* . . . . chrysanthemum
jùyuàn *(joo-we-yoo-ahn)* . . . . theater
júzishuǐ *(joo-zuh-shway)* . . . . orange juice

K

kāfēi *(kah-fay)* . . . . coffee
kāfēi diàn *(kah-fay)(dee-ahn)* . . . . coffee shop
kāfēisè *(kah-fay-suh)* . . . . brown (coffee-colored)
kāi *(ki)* . . . . to open, open, opens
kāi *(ki)* . . . . to leave, depart, departure
kàn *(kahn)* . . . . to read (books), look at
kànjiàn *(kahn-jee-ahn)* . . . . to see, sees, see
kǎo *(kow)* . . . . broiled, baked
kètīng *(kuh-teeng)* . . . . living room
kǒuqín *(koh-cheen)* . . . . harmonica
kuài *(kwhy)* . . . . fast, unit of Chinese money
kuàichē *(kwhy-chuh)* . . . . fast train
kuàizi *(kwhy-zuh)* . . . . chopsticks
kuàngquán shuǐ *(kwahng-choo-ahn)(shway)* . . . mineral water
kùwà *(koo-wah)* . . . . pantyhose
kùzi *(koo-zuh)* . . . . trousers

L

lā *(lah)* . . . . to pull
là *(lah)* . . . . wax
làbǐ *(lah-bee)* . . . . crayon
lái *(lie)* . . . . to come, come, comes
láihuí *(lie-hway)* . . . . round-trip
lán *(lahn)* . . . . blue
lán bǎoshí *(lahn)(bao-shr)* . . . . sapphire
lánhuā *(lahn-hwah)* . . . . orchid

lǎo *(lao)* . . . . old
Lǎowō *(lao-woh)* . . . . Laos
làtái *(lah-tie)* . . . . candlestick
làzhǐ *(lah-jihr)* . . . . wax paper
làzhú *(lah-joo)* . . . . candle
le *(luh)* . . . . with a verb indicating completed action
lěng *(lung)* . . . . cold
lěngpán *(lung-pahn)* . . . . appetizers
lǐ *(lee)* . . . . inside
liǎng *(lee-ahng)* . . . . two
liàng *(lee-ahng)* . . . . measure word (M)
liǎngbǎi *(lee-ahng-by)* . . . . two hundred
liángxié *(lee-ahng-ssee-eh)* . . . . sandals
liányīqún *(lee-ahn-yee-choon)* . . . . dress
lièjiǔ *(lee-eh-jee-oo)* . . . . spirits (alcohol)
lǐfà diàn *(lee-fah)(dee-ahn)* . . . . hairdresser's
lǐfàguǎn *(lee-fah-gwahn)* . . . . barber shop
líng *(leeng)* . . . . zero
lǐngdài *(leeng-die)* . . . . tie
língqián *(leeng-chee-ahn)* . . . . change (money)
línyù *(leen-yoo-we)* . . . . shower
lìshǐ *(lee-shr)* . . . . history
liù *(lee-oo)* . . . . six
liùbǎi *(lee-oo-by)* . . . . six hundred
liùshí *(lee-oo-shr)* . . . . sixty
liùyī értóng jié *(lee-oo-yee)(ur-tohng)(jee-eh)* . . . .
. . . . Children's Day (June 1)
liùyuè *(lee-oo-yoo-eh)* . . . . June
lóu *(loh)* . . . . floor
lù *(loo)* . . . . road, route
lǜ *(loo-we)* . . . . green
lǚguǎn *(loo-we-gwahn)* . . . . hotel
lǚguǎn de chāntīng *(loo-we-gwahn)(duh)(chahn-teeng)* . . . .
. . . . hotel café
lǚguǎn jīnglǐ *(loo-we-gwahn)(jeeng-lee)* . . . . . hotel manager
lǚkè *(loo-we-kuh)* . . . . passenger, traveler, tourist
lǜsè *(loo-we-suh)* . . . . green-colored
lǚxíng *(loo-we-sseng)* . . . . to travel, travels, travel
lǚxíng shè *(loo-we-sseng)(shuh)* . travel agent, travel agency
lǚxíng zhīpiào *(loo-we-sseng)(jihr-pee-ow)* . . traveler's checks
lúzi *(loo-zuh)* . . . . stove

M

ma *(mah)* . . . . used at end of yes-no questions
mā *(mah)* . . . . mother
má *(mah)* . . . . hemp
mǎ *(mah)* . . . . horse
mà *(mah)* . . . . curse
mǎi *(my)* . . . . to buy, buys, buy
mài *(my)* . . . . to sell, sells, sell
mǎmǎhūhū *(mah-mah-hoo-hoo)* . . . . so-so
màn *(mahn)* . . . . slow
màn man *(mahn)(mahn)* . . . . slowly
māo *(mao)* . . . . cat
máo *(mao)* . . . . wool, unit of Chinese money
máobǐ *(mao-bee)* . . . . writing brush
máojīn *(mao-jeen)* . . . . towel
máopí *(mao-pee)* . . . . fur
máoyī *(mao-yee)* . . . . sweater
màozi *(mao-zuh)* . . . . hat
máquè *(mah-choo-eh)* . . . . sparrow
mǎtǒng *(mah-twong)* . . . . toilet
méi *(may)* . . . . coal
méi yǒu *(may)(yoh)* . . . . have not had
méiguìhuā *(may-gway-hwah)* . . . . rose
Měiguó *(may-gwoh)* . . . . the United States
méikuàng *(may-kwahng)* . . . . coal mine

111

mèimei (may-may) . . . . (younger) sister
méiqì (may-chee) . . . . gas
méiqìlú (may-chee-loo) . . . . gas stove
měishùguǎn (may-shoo-gwahn) . . . . art gallery
méiyóu (may-yoh) . . . . kerosene
mén (muhn) . . . . door, gate
Měnggǔ (muhng-goo) . . . . Mongolia
mǐ (mee) . . . . rice
mì (mee) . . . . honey
miàn (mee-ahn) . . . . noodles
miàn fàn (mee-ahn)(fahn) . . . . noodles and rice dishes
miàn guǎn (mee-ahn)(gwahn) . . . . noodle shop
miànbāo (mee-ahn-bao) . . . . bread
miànbāo diàn (mee-ahn-bao)(dee-ahn) . . . . bakery
miànbāochē (mee-ahn-bao-chuh) . . . . van
miǎo (mee-ow) . . . . second
miào (mee-ow) . . . . temple
mǐfàn (mee-fahn) . . . . cooked rice
mǐfěn (mee-fuhn) . . . . rice noodle
mìfēng (mee-fung) . . . . honeybee
mìjiàn (mee-jee-ahn) . . . . candied fruit
mǐjiǔ (mee-jee-oo) . . . . rice wine
mìjú (mee-joo) . . . . tangerine
míng nián (meeng)(nee-ahn) . . . . next year
míngtiān (meeng-tee-ahn) . . . . tomorrow
míngtiān jiàn (meeng-tee-ahn)(jee-ahn) . . see you tomorrow
míngxìnpiàn (meeng-sseen-pee-ahn) . . . . postcard
míngzì (meeng-zih) . . . . name
mǐsè (mee-suh) . . . . cream-colored
mìyuè (mee-yoo-eh) . . . . honeymoon
mǔqin (moo-cheen) . . . . mother

N

nǎ (nah) . . . . which
nà (nah) . . . . that, those
nán (nahn) . . . . male
nán (nahn) . . . . south
nánbiān (nahn-bee-ahn) . . . . South
nánfāng (nahn-fahng) . . . . southern
Nánfēi (nahn-fay) . . . . South Africa
nánrén (nahn-ruhn) . . . . man, men
nánzhuāng (nahn-jwahng) . . . . men's clothing
nàozhōng (now-jwong) . . . . alarm clock
nǎr (nahr) . . . . where
náshǒucài (nah-shoh-tsi) . . . . specialties (food)
něi (nay) . . . . which
nèikù (nay-koo) . . . . underpants
nèiyī (nay-yee) . . . . undershirt
néng (nung) . . . . to be able to, can
nǐ (nee) . . . . you
Nǐ hǎo ma? (nee)(how)(mah) . . . . How are you?
Nǐ jiào shénme míngzì? (nee)(jee-ow)(shun-muh)
(meeng-zuh) . . . . How are you called?, What is your name?
nián (nee-ahn) . . . . year
niánqīng (nee-ahn-cheeng) . . . . young
niǎo (nee-ow) . . . . bird
niǎolóng (nee-ow-lwong) . . . . birdcage
nǐde (nee-duh) . . . . your
nǐmen (nee-muhn) . . . . . . you (as in you all, you guys)
nín zǎo (neen)(zow) . . . . good morning
nǐnhǎo (neen-how) . . . . hello
niú (nee-oo) . . . . cow
niúdú (nee-oo-doo) . . . . calf
niújiǎo (nee-oo-jee-ow) . . . . horn
niúnǎi (nee-oo-ni) . . . . milk
niúnǎi diàn (nee-oo-ni)(dee-ahn) . . . . dairy
112 niúpái (nee-oo-pie) . . . . beefsteak

niúpí (nee-oo-pee) . . . . leather
niúpí zhǐ (nee-oo-pee)(jihr) . . . . brown paper
niúròu (nee-oo-roh) . . . . beef
niúwěi (nee-oo-way) . . . . oxtail
niúyóu (nee-oo-yoh) . . . . butter
niúzǎikù (nee-oo-zi-koo) . . . . jeans
nǚ (noo-we) . . . . female
nuǎnhuo (noo-ahn-hwoh) . . . . warm
nǚér (noo-we-ur) . . . . daughter
Nuówēi (nwoh-way) . . . . Norway
nǚrén (noo-we-ruhn) . . . . woman, women
nǚzhuāng (noo-we-jwahng) . . . . women's clothing

O

Ōuzhōu (oh-joh) . . . . Europe

P

pán (pahn) . . . . plate, portion (M)
pángbiān (pahng-bee-ahn) . . . . next to
pánzi (pahn-zuh) . . . . plate
péngyou (pung-yoh) . . . . friend
piányí (pee-ahn-yee) . . . . inexpensive
piào (pee-ow) . . . . ticket
píbāo (pee-bao) . . . . purse, handbag
píjiāzi (pee-jee-ah-zuh) . . . . wallet
píjiǔ (pee-jee-oo) . . . . beer
píng (peeng) . . . . bottle
píngguǒ (peeng-gwoh) . . . . apple
píngguǒyuán (peeng-gwoh-yoo-ahn) . . . . apple orchard
pízhì pǐn (pee-jihr)(peen) . . . . leather
pǔtōngchē (poo-tohng-chuh) . . . . ordinary train
pǔtōnghuà (poo-tohng-hwah) . . . . common language

Q

qī (chee) . . . . seven
qí (chee) . . . . to ride
qián (chee-ahn) . . . . money
qiānbǐ (chee-ahn-bee) . . . . pencil
qiánbiān (chee-ahn-bee-ahn) . . . . in front of
qiángjiǎo (chee-ahng-jee-ow) . . . . corner
qiānzhèng (chee-ahn-jung) . . . . visa
qībǎi (chee-by) . . . . seven hundred
qìchē (chee-chuh) . . . . car
qiè wù rùnèi (chee-eh)(woo)(roo-nay) . . . . keep out
qín (cheen) . . . . musical instrument
qíncài (cheen-tsi) . . . . celery
qǐng (cheeng) . . . . please
qīngcài (cheeng-tsi) . . . . green vegetables
qǐngwèn (cheeng-wuhn) . . . . excuse me, may I ask
qióng (chee-wong) . . . . poor
qīshí (chee-shr) . . . . seventy
qiūtiān (chee-yoo-tee-ahn) . . . . autumn
qiúxié (chee-yoo-ssee-eh) . . . . sport shoes
qìwēn (chee-wuhn) . . . . temperature
qīyuè (chee-yoo-eh) . . . . July
qù (chee-oo) . . . . to go (to, into), go, goes
qù nián (chee-oo)(nee-ahn) . . . . last year
qúnzi (choon-zuh) . . . . skirt

R

rè (ruh) . . . . hot
rén (ruhn) . . . . person
rénkǒu (ruhn-koh) . . . . population
rénlèi (ruhn-lay) . . . . mankind
rénlì (ruhn-lee) . . . . manpower
rénmen (ruhn-muhn) . . . . people
rénqún (ruhn-choon) . . . . crowd

rénxíngdào (*ruhn-ssseng-dow*) . . . . sidewalk
rénzào (*ruhn-zow*) . . . . man-made
rénzhǒng (*ruhn-jwong*) . . . . human race
Rìběn (*ree-buhn*) . . . . Japan
rìlì (*rur-lee*) . . . . calendar
Rìwén (*ree-wuhn*) . . . . Japanese
róngyì (*rohng-yee*) . . . . easy
ròu (*roh*) . . . . meat
ròu diàn (*roh*)(*dee-ahn*) . . . . butcher shop
rùkǒu (*roo-koh*) . . . . entrance

S

sān (*sahn*) . . . . three
sǎn (*sahn*) . . . . umbrella
sān nián (*sahn*)(*nee-ahn*) . . . . three years
sānbǎi (*sahn-by*) . . . . three hundred
sānlúnchē (*sahn-loon-chuh*) . . . . pedicab
sānshí (*sahn-shr*) . . . . thirty
sānyuè (*sahn-yoo-eh*) . . . . March
sèlā (*suh-lah*) . . . . salad
shāfā (*shah-fah*) . . . . sofa
shàng (*shahng*) . . . . up, on, on top of
shàngbiān (*shahng-bee-ahn*) . . . . over, above
shāngdiàn (*shahng-dee-ahn*) . . . . store
shàngwǔ (*shahng-woo*) . . . . morning
shàngyī (*shahng-yee*) . . . . jacket, upper outer garment
shāo (*shao*) . . . . roasted
shǎo (*shao*) . . . . little, few
shéi (*shay*) . . . . who
shēngcài (*shuhng-tsi*) . . . . lettuce
shénme (*shun-muh*) . . . . what
shénme dìfāng (*shun-muh*)(*dee-fahng*) . . what place, where
shénme rén (*shun-muh*)(*ruhn*) . . . . what person, who
shénme shíhou (*shun-muh*)(*shr-hoh*) . . . . when, what time
shèshì (*shuh-shr*) . . . . Centigrade
shí (*shr*) . . . . stone, rock
shí (*shr*) . . . . ten
shì (*shr*) . . . . to be, am, is, are
shì (*shr*) . . . . yes
shíbā (*shr-bah*) . . . . eighteen
shídiāo (*shr-dee-ow*) . . . . carved stone
shíèr (*shr-ur*) . . . . twelve
shíèryuè (*shr-ur-yoo-eh*) . . . . December
shìhé (*shr-huh*) . . . . it fits
shíjiān (*shr-jee-ahn*) . . . . time
shíjiān biǎo (*shr-jee-ahn*)(*bee-ow*) . . . . hours, time schedule
shíjiǔ (*shr-jee-oo*) . . . . nineteen
shíkuài (*shr-kwhy*) . . . . boulder
shíliù (*shr-lee-oo*) . . . . sixteen
shímò (*shr-mwoh*) . . . . graphite
shípǐn diàn (*shr-peen*)(*dee-ahn*) . . . . grocery store
shípǔ (*shr-poo*) . . . . cookbook, recipes
shíqī (*shr-chee*) . . . . seventeen
shísān (*shr-sahn*) . . . . thirteen
shísì (*shr-sih*) . . . . fourteen
shísù (*shr-soo*) . . . . room and board
shíwǔ (*shr-woo*) . . . . fifteen
shíwù (*shr-woo*) . . . . food
shíwǔ fēn (*shr-woo*)(*fuhn*) . . fifteen minutes, a quarter (time)
shīwù zhāolǐng (*shr-woo*)(*jow-leeng*) . . lost-and-found office
shíyī (*shr-yee*) . . . . eleven
shíyīng (*shr-yeeng*) . . . . quartz
shíyīyuè (*shr-yee-yoo-eh*) . . . . November
shíyù (*shr-yoo-we*) . . . . appetite
shíyuè (*shr-yoo-eh*) . . . . October
shízhǐ (*shr-jihr*) . . . . index finger
shōu (*shoh*) . . . . to take, accept

shōujù (*shoh-joo*) . . . . receipt
shǒujuàn (*shoh-joo-ahn*) . . . . handkerchief
shòupiào chù (*shoh-pee-ow*)(*choo*) . . . . ticket office
shòupiàoyuán (*shoh-pee-ow-yoo-ahn*) . . ticket seller, conductor
shōushi (*shwoh-shr*) . . . . to pack
shǒutào (*shoh-tao*) . . . . gloves
shū (*shoo*) . . . . book
shuāngrénfáng (*shwahng-ruhn-fahng*) . . . . . . double room
shūbāo (*shoo-bao*) . . . . bookbag
shūbāo tān (*shoo-bao*)(*tahn*) . . . . bookstand
shúcài (*shoo-tsi*) . . . . vegetables
shūchú (*shoo-choo*) . . . . bookcase
shūdiàn (*shoo-dee-ahn*) . . . . bookstore
shūfǎ (*shoo-fah*) . . . . handwriting, calligraphy
shūfáng (*shoo-fahng*) . . . . study, den
shūjià (*shoo-jee-ah*) . . . . bookshelf
shuǐ (*shway*) . . . . water
shuì (*shway*) . . . . to sleep
shuì gè hǎo jiào (*shway*)(*guh*)(*how*)(*jee-ow*) . . . . sleep well!
shuǐbà (*shway-bah*) . . . . dam
shuǐcǎi (*shway-tsi*) . . . . watercolor
shuǐchē (*shway-chuh*) . . . . watermill
shuǐchí (*shway-chr*) . . . . pool
shuìfáng (*shway-fahng*) . . . . bedroom
shuǐfèn (*shway-fuhn*) . . . . moisture
shuǐguǒ (*shway-gwoh*) . . . . fresh fruit
shuǐguǒ diàn (*shway-gwoh*)(*dee-ahn*) . . . . fruit store
shuǐkù (*shway-koo*) . . . . reservoir
shuìpáo (*shway-pow*) . . . . bathrobe
shuǐpíng (*shway-peeng*) . . . . water bottle
shuǐshǒu (*shway-shwoh*) . . . . sailor
shuìyī (*shway-yee*) . . . . nightshirt, pajamas
shuǐzāi (*shway-zi*) . . . . flood
shuǐzúguǎn (*shway-zoo-gwahn*) . . . . aquarium
shuō (*shwoh*) . . . . to say, speak
shuōhuà (*shwoh-hwah*) . . . . speaking
shūpíng (*shoo-peeng*) . . . . book review
shūqiān (*shoo-chee-ahn*) . . . . bookmark
shúshí diàn (*shoo-shr*)(*dee-ahn*) . . . . delicatessen
shūshu (*shoo-shoo*) . . . . uncle
shūzhuō (*shoo-jwoh*) . . . . desk
shūzi (*shoo-zuh*) . . . . comb
shùzì (*shoo-zih*) . . . . number
sī (*sih*) . . . . silk
sì (*sih*) . . . . four
sìbǎi (*sih-by*) . . . . four hundred
sìshí (*sih-shr*) . . . . forty
sìyuè (*sih-yoo-eh*) . . . . April

T

tā (*tah*) . . . . he, she, it, him, her
táidēng (*tie-dung*) . . . . table lamp
Tàiguó (*tie-gwoh*) . . . . Thailand
tàipíng mén (*tie-peeng*)(*muhn*) . . . . emergency gate
tàitai (*tie-tie*) . . . . Mrs.
tàiyáng (*tie-yahng*) . . . . sun
tàiyáng yǎnjìng (*tie-yahng*)(*yahn-jeeng*) . . . . sunglasses
tāmen (*tah-muhn*) . . . . they, them
tāng (*tahng*) . . . . soup
tāngchí (*tahng-chr*) . . . . soup spoon
tǎngyǐ (*tahng-yee*) . . . . reclining seats, recliner, reclining car
tāngyuán (*tahng-yoo-ahn*) . . . . sweet rice-flour ball
tèbié (*tuh-bee-uh*) . . . . especially
tī (*tee*) . . . . ladder
tí (*tee*) . . . . to lift
tǐ (*tee*) . . . . body
tì (*tee*) . . . . tears **113**

tiān (tee-ahn) . . . . day
tiándiǎn (tee-ahn-dee-ahn) . . . . dessert
tiānqì (tee-ahn-chee) . . . . weather
tiāntiān (tee-ahn-tee-ahn) . . . . everyday
tiānwéntái (tee-ahn-wuhn-tie) . . . . observatory
tiānzhǔjiào (tee-ahn-joo-jee-ow) . . . . Catholic
tiáo (tee-ow) . . . . measure word (M)
tiěguǐ (tee-eh-gway) . . . . track
tīng (teeng) . . . . listen to
tíng (teeng) . . . . booth
tíngchē chǎng (teeng-chuh)(chahng) . . . . parking lot
tíngliú (teeng-lee-oo) . . . . to stay, stays, stay
tīngtǒng (teeng-tohng) . . . . receiver
tíqín (tee-cheen) . . . . violin
tǐyùguǎn (tee-yoo-we-gwahn) . . . . gymnasium
tóu děng (toh)(dung) . . . . first class
tú (too) . . . . disciple
tuī (tway) . . . . to push
tuōxié (twoh-ssee-eh) . . . . slippers
túshūguǎn (too-shoo-gwahn) . . . . library

W

wàiguó (why-gwoh) . . . . foreign
wàitào (why-tao) . . . . jacket
wǎn (wahn) . . . . evening, night
wǎn ān (wahn)(ahn) . . . . good night
wǎnfàn (wahn-fahn) . . . . dinner, supper
wánjù (wahn-joo) . . . . toys
wǎnshàng (wahn-shahng) . . . . evening
wǎnshàng jiàn (wahn-shahng)(jee-ahn) . . see you in the evening
wàzi (wah-zuh) . . . . socks
wèi (way) . . . . hey, hello
wèishēngzhǐ (way-shung-jihr) . . . . toilet paper
wèishénme (way-shun-muh) . . . . why
wén (wuhn) . . . . written language
wèn (wuhn) . . . . to ask, asks, ask
wénhuàshān (wuhn-hwah-shahn) . . . . T-shirt
wénjiàn (wuhn-jee-ahn) . . . . documents
wénjù (wuhn-joo-we) . . . . stationery
wénjù diàn (wuhn-joo-we)(dee-ahn) . . . . stationery store
wèntí (wuhn-tee) . . . . question
wǒ (woh) . . . . I, me
wǒ è le (woh)(uh)(luh) . . . . I'm hungry
wǒ kǒu kě (woh)(koh)(kuh) . . . . I'm thirsty
wǒ mílù le (woh)(mee-loo)(luh) . . . . I'm lost
wǒ shì (woh)(shr) . . . . I am
wǒ zài (woh)(zi) . . . . I am (in, at)
wǒde (woh-duh) . . . . my
wǒmen (woh-muhn) . . . . we, us
wòpù (woh-poo) . . . . sleeping car
wǔ (woo) . . . . five
wǔbǎi (woo-by) . . . . five hundred
wǔfàn (woo-fahn) . . . . lunch, mid-day meal
wǔqiān (woo-chee-ahn) . . . . five thousand
wǔshí (woo-shr) . . . . fifty
wūyā (woo-yah) . . . . crow
wǔyè (woo-yeh) . . . . midnight
wǔyī láodòng jié (woo-yee)(lao-dohng)(jee-eh) . . . .
. . . . Labor Day (May 1)
wǔyuè (woo-yoo-eh) . . . . May

X

xī (ssee) . . . . west
xǐ (ssee) . . . . to wash, washes, wash
xià (ssee-ah) . . . . down
114 xiàbiān (ssee-ah-bee-ahn) . . . . under, below

xiàbiānde (ssee-ah-bee-ahn-duh) . . . . below
xiàn (ssee-ah) . . . . line
xiàng (ssee-ahng) . . . . to want, wants, want
xiǎng yào (ssee-ahng)(yow) . . . . would like
xiānshēng (ssee-ahn-shuhng) . . . . Mr., sir
xiāngzi (ssee-ahng-zuh) . . . . trunk, suitcase
xiànzài (ssee-ahn-zi) . . . . now
xiǎo (ssee-ow) . . . . small
xiǎo chīdiàn (ssee-ow)(chr-dee-ahn) . . . . snack shop
xiǎohái (ssee-ow-hi) . . . . child, children
xiǎojiě (ssee-ow-jee-eh) . . . . Miss
xiǎoshí (ssee-ow-shr) . . . . hour
xiāròu hún tūn (ssee-ah-roh)(hoon)(toon) . . . .
. . . . shrimp and vegetables in a wrapper, boiled
xiàtiān (ssee-ah-tee-ahn) . . . . summer
xiàwǔ (ssee-ah-woo) . . . . afternoon
xiàxuě (ssee-ah-ssee-yoo-eh) . . . . to snow, snow, snows
xiàyǔ (ssee-ah-yoo-we) . . . . to rain, rain, rains
Xībānyá (ssee-bahn-yah) . . . . Spain
xīběi (ssee-bay) . . . . west-north
xībiān (ssee-bee-ahn) . . . . West
xiē (ssee-eh) . . . . several
xié (ssee-eh) . . . . shoes
xiě (ssee-eh) . . . . to write
xiě chū (ssee-eh)(choo) . . . . to write out
xié diàn (ssee-eh)(dee-ahn) . . . . shoe store
xièxie (ssee-eh-ssee-eh) . . . . thank you
xīfāng (ssee-fahng) . . . . western
xǐhuān (ssee-hoo-ahn) . . . . to like
xǐjiāojuǎn (ssee-jee-ow-joo-ahn) . . . . . . to develop (the) film
xǐliǎnpén (ssee-lee-ahn-puhn) . . . . washbasin
xīn (sseen) . . . . new
xìn (sseen) . . . . letter
xínglǐ (sseeng-lee) . . . . luggage, baggage
xínglǐ chē (sseeng-lee)(chuh) . . . . baggage cart
xīngqī (sseeng-chee) . . . . week
xīngqīèr (sseeng-chee-ur) . . . . Tuesday
xīngqīliù (sseeng-chee-lee-oo) . . . . Saturday
xīngqīsān (sseeng-chee-sahn) . . . . Wednesday
xīngqīsì (sseeng-chee-sih) . . . . Thursday
xīngqītiān (sseeng-chee-tee-ahn) . . . . Sunday
xīngqīwǔ (sseeng-chee-woo) . . . . Friday
xīngqīyī (sseeng-chee-yee) . . . . Monday
Xīnxīlán (sseen-ssee-lahn) . . . . New Zealand
xìnyòngkǎ (sseen-yohng-kah) . . . . credit card
xiōngzhào (ssee-wong-jow) . . . . bra
xìpiào (ssee-pee-ow) . . . . theater ticket
xǐyī diàn (ssee-yee)(dee-ahn) . . . . laundry
xǐyīfú (ssee-yee-foo) . . . . to do laundry
xìyuàn (ssee-yoo-ahn) . . . . theater
xǐzǎo (ssee-zow) . . . . to bathe
xīzhuāng (ssee-jwahng) . . . . suit
xuěhuā (ssee-oo-eh-hwah) . . . . snowflake
xuéxí (ssee-yoo-eh-ssee) . . . . . . to learn, learns, learn
xuéxiào (ssee-yoo-eh-ssee-ow) . . . . school
xuēzi (ssee-yoo-eh-zuh) . . . . boots
xūyào (ssee-oo-yow) . . . . to need, needs, need

Y

yā (yah) . . . . duck
yágāo (yah-gow) . . . . toothpaste
yán (yahn) . . . . salt
yángròu (yahng-roh) . . . . mutton
yǎnjìng (yahn-jeeng) . . . . eyeglasses
yánsè (yahn-suh) . . . . color
yào (yow) . . . . want, must
yào (yow) . . . . to take (time)

yào diàn *(yow)(dee-ahn)*	pharmacy
yáoyǐ *(yow-yee)*	rocking chair
yáshuā *(yah-shwah)*	toothbrush
yě *(yuh)*	also
yè *(yeh)*	page
yèlǐ *(yeh-lee)*	night
yī, yì, yí *(yee)*	one
yī *(yee)*	clothing
yǐ *(yee)*	chair
Yí lù píng ān! *(yee)(loo)(peeng)(ahn)*	safe and peaceful journey
yí xià *(yee)(ssee-ah)*	a little while
yìbǎi *(yee-by)*	one hundred
yīchú *(yee-choo)*	clothes closet
Yìdàlì *(yee-dah-lee)*	Italy
yìdiǎn *(yee-dee-ahn)*	a little
yīfu *(yee-foo)*	clothes
yígòng *(yee-gohng)*	altogether
Yìndù *(yeen-doo)*	India
Yìndùníxīyà *(yeen-doo-nee-ssee-yah)*	Indonesia
yīng *(yeeng)*	eagle
yīnggāi *(yeeng-gi)*	to have to, should
Yīngguó *(yeeng-gwoh)*	England
Yīngguó rén *(yeeng-gwoh)(ruhn)*	British
yīngwǔ *(yeeng-woo)*	parrot
Yīngwén *(yeeng-wuhn)*	English
yínháng *(yeen-hahng)*	bank
yǐnliào *(yeen-lee-ow)*	beverages
yínqì *(yeen-chee)*	silver
yìqiān *(yee-chee-ahn)*	one thousand
yīshēng *(yee-shuhng)*	doctor
yíyàng *(yee-yahng)*	same
yīyuàn *(yee-yoo-ahn)*	hospital
yīyuè *(yee-yoo-eh)*	January
yǐzi *(yee-zuh)*	chair
yìzhí zǒu *(yee-jihr)(zoh)*	straight ahead
yǒu *(yoh)*	to have, has, have
yǒu *(yoh)*	there is, there are
yòu *(yoh)*	right
yòubiān *(yoh-bee-ahn)*	right side
yóujú *(yoh-joo-we)*	post office
yóupiào *(yoh-pee-ow)*	stamp
yǒuqián *(yoh-chee-ahn)*	rich
yǒurén *(yoh-ruhn)*	occupied
yóutǒng *(yoh-twong)*	mailbox
yǒuyìsi *(yoh-yee-see)*	interesting
yóuyǒngyī *(yoh-yohng-yee)*	swimsuit
yóuzhèng *(yoh-jung)*	postal
yú *(yoo-we)*	fish
yú diàn *(yoo-we)(dee-ahn)*	fish store
yuán *(yoo-ahn)*	unit of Chinese currency
yuánzhūbǐ *(yoo-ahn-joo-bee)*	ballpoint pen
yuè *(yoo-eh)*	month
yuèbào *(yoo-eh-bao)*	monthly magazine
yuèliang *(yoo-eh-lee-ahng)*	moon
Yuènán *(yoo-eh-nahn)*	Vietnam
yuèsè *(yoo-eh-suh)*	moonlight
yuètái *(yoo-eh-tie)*	platform
yuèyè *(yoo-eh-yeh)*	moonlit night
yùgāng *(yoo-we-gahng)*	bath
yùndòng yòngpǐn *(yoon-dohng)(yohng-peen)*	sporting goods
yùndòngxié *(yoon-dohng-ssee-eh)*	tennis shoes
yùshì *(yoo-we-shr)*	bathroom
yǔyī *(yoo-we-yee)*	raincoat
yùyuē *(yoo-we-yoo-eh)*	reservation

Z

zài *(zi)*	is, are (in, at)
zài shuō yíbiàn *(zi)(shwoh)(yee-bee-ahn)*	to say again, repeat once again
zài yòubiān *(zi)(yoh-bee-ahn)*	on the right side
zài zuǒbiān *(zi)(zwoh-bee-ahn)*	on the left side
zàijiàn *(zi-jee-ahn)*	good-bye, see you again
zǎofàn *(zow-fahn)*	breakfast
zázhì *(zah-jihr)*	magazine
zěnme *(zuhn-muh)*	how
zěnme yàng *(zuhn-muh)(yahng)*	how
zhá *(jah)*	deep-fried
zhàn *(jahn)*	stop, station
zhāng *(jahng)*	sheet, flat (M)
zhàng *(jahng)*	account, bill
zhàngdān *(jahng-dahn)*	bill
zhǎnlǎnguǎn *(jahn-lahn-gwahn)*	exhibition hall
zhǎo *(jow)*	to look for
zhàopiàn *(jow-pee-ahn)*	photo
zhàoxiàng yòngpǐn *(jow-ssee-ahng)(yohng-peen)*	cameras
zhàoxiàngjī *(jow-ssee-ahng-jee)*	camera
zhè *(juh)*	this, these
zhèi *(juh-ay)*	this, these
zhēng *(jung)*	steamed
zhèngquède *(jung-choo-eh-duh)*	correct
zhěntóu *(juhn-toh)*	pillow
zhèr *(juhr)*	here
zhèxiē *(juh-ssee-eh)*	these
zhǐ *(jihr)*	paper
zhǐ *(jihr)*	only
zhǐbì *(jihr-bee)*	paper currency
zhīdào *(jihr-dow)*	to know, knows, know
zhōng *(jwong)*	clock
zhōngbiǎo *(jwong-bee-ow)*	clocks and watches
zhōngbiǎo diàn *(jwong-bee-ow)(dee-ahn)*	watchmaker's
Zhōngguó *(jwong-gwoh)*	China
Zhōngguóde *(jwong-gwoh-duh)*	Chinese
Zhōngwén *(jwong-wuhn)*	Chinese language
zhōngwǔ *(jwong-woo)*	noon
zhōngyāng gōngyuán *(jwong-yahng)(gohng-yoo-ahn)*	central park
zhòngyào *(jwong-yow)*	important
zhǔ *(joo)*	boiled
zhù *(joo)*	to live, reside
zhù nǐ shùnlì *(joo)(nee)(shoon-lee)*	wish you good luck
zhuǎn *(jwahn)*	to turn
zhuànyǐ *(jwahn-yee)*	swivel chair
zhūbǎo *(joo-bao)*	jewelry
zhuōzi *(jwoh-zuh)*	table
zhūròu *(joo-roh)*	pork
zì *(zih)*	Chinese character
zìdiǎn *(zih-dee-ahn)*	character dictionary
zìtiáo *(zih-tee-ow)*	note
zìmǔ *(zih-moo)*	letters of the alphabet
zìmù *(zih-moo)*	subtitles
zìxíngchē *(zih-sseeng-chuh)*	bicycle
zìzhǐlóu *(zih-jihr-loh)*	wastepaper basket
zōngjiào *(zwong-jee-ow)*	religion
zòngzi *(zwong-zuh)*	stuffed, sweet rice
zuànshí *(zwahn-shr)*	diamond
zǔfù *(zoo-foo)*	grandfather
zǔfùmǔ *(zoo-foo-moo)*	grandparents
zǔmǔ *(zoo-moo)*	grandmother
zuǒ *(zwoh)*	left
zuò *(zwoh)*	by, via
zuò *(zwoh)*	to sit, ride in
zuǒbiān *(zwoh-bee-ahn)*	left side
zuótiān *(zwoh-tee-ahn)*	yesterday
zuòwèi *(zwoh-way)*	seat

This beverage guide is intended to explain the variety of beverages available to you while **zài Zhōngguó.** It is by no means complete. Some of the experimenting has been left up to you, but this should get you started.

Chá (tea)

hóng chá . . . . black tea
   lìzhī hóng chá . . . . . . litchi black tea

hóng chá jiā niúnǎi . . tea with milk
níngméng chá . . . . tea with lemon
lǜ chá . . . . green tea
wūlóng chá . . . . fermented tea
mòlìhuà chá . . . . jasmine tea
qīng chá . . . . plain tea

Jiǔ (wine)

pútáojiǔ . . . . grape wine
hóng pútáojiǔ . . . . red wine
bái pútáojiǔ . . . . white wine
huángjiǔ . . . . rice wine from
                      Shàoxīng area
xiāngbīn . . . . champagne

Píjiǔ (beer)

hēi píjiǔ . . . . black beer

(gahn-bay)
Gānbēi!
cheers

Lièjiǔ (spirits)

báilándì . . . . brandy
wēishìjì . . . . whisky
lǎngmǔjiǔ . . . . rum
fútèjiā . . . . vodka
dùsōngzǐjiǔ . . . . gin
gāoliángjiǔ . . . . sorghum spirits
zhúyèqīng . . . . very strong Chinese
                      spirits
lǜdào shāojiǔ . . . . very strong spirits
máotáijiǔ . . . . spirits from
                      Guìzhōu area
fénjiǔ . . . . spirits from
                      Shānxī area

Qítā Yǐnliào (other beverages)

lěng yǐn . . . . cold drink
qìshuǐ . . . . soft drink, lemonade
kuàngquán shuǐ . . . . . mineral water
sūdǎshuǐ . . . . soda water
kāishuǐ . . . . boiled water
shuǐguǒ zhī . . . . fruit juice
júzishuǐ . . . . orange juice
píngguǒ zhī . . . . apple juice
kěkǒukělè . . . . Coca Cola
bǎishì kělè . . . . Pepsi Cola
kāfēi . . . . coffee
kāfēi jiā niúnǎi . . . . . . coffee with cream
niúnǎi . . . . milk
lěng niúnǎi . . . . cold milk
kěkě . . . . cocoa
rè qiǎokèlì . . . . hot chocolate
suān méi tāng . . . . soft drink (made
                      from dried prunes,
                      sugar and spices)

Bīngkuài . . . . ice cubes

Càidān
menu guide

菜单

Zuò Fǎ (ways of preparation)
做法

miàntuō	in batter
zhǔ	boiled
kǎo	baked
shāo	roasted
zhēng	steamed
zhá	fried, deep-fried
chǎo	stir-fried, sautéd
kǎo	broiled

Shuǐguǒ (fruit)
水果

júzi	orange
lǐzi	plum, pear
táozi	peach
xiāngjiāo	banana
mìjú	tangerine
mángguǒ	mango
wúhuāguǒ	fig
lìzhī	litchi
yīngtáo	cherries
píngguǒ	apple
méizi	prune
pútáo	grapes
zǎozi	dates
níngméng	lemon
cǎoméi	strawberries
mùméi	raspberries
xìngzi	apricot
yēzi	coconut
shìzi	persimmon
bōluó	pineapple

Diǎnxīn (snacks)
点心

dòu shā bāo	steamed bun with red-bean paste
cài bāo	steamed bun with vegetables
zhī má bǐng	sesame crisp cake
bāsī píngguǒ	hot-candied apple

Miàn Fàn (rice and noodles)
面饭

bái fàn	plain rice
dàn chǎo fàn	fried rice with egg
jīsī miàn	noodles with shredded chicken
ròusī miàn	noodles with shredded pork
xiārén miàn	noodles with shrimp
dōnggū miàn	noodles with mushrooms
zhūgān miàn	noodles with pork liver
sùcài miàn	noodles with vegetables
chǎo miàn	fried noodles
xiārén chǎo miàn	fried noodles with shrimp

Chīfàn
(chr-fahn)
let's eat

Shūcài (vegetables)
蔬菜

dòuyá	bean sprouts
càihuā	cauliflower
sǔn	bamboo sprouts
cōng	green onions
jiāng	ginger
qíncài	celery
báicài	cabbage
bōcài	spinach
mógū	mushrooms
huángguā	cucumbers
biǎndòu	beans
wāndòu	peas
shēngcài	lettuce

Lěng Pán (appetizers)
冷盘

bái qiē jī	cold chicken
wǔxiāng yā	spicy duck
yóu bào xiā	oil-fried shrimps
xūn yú	smoked fish
wǔxiāng niúròu	spiced beef
xián dàn	pickled salted egg
yánshuǐ yā	salted duck
bàn hǎizhé	fish jelly
là cài	hot, pickled mustard greens
xián huā shēng	salted peanuts

Tāng (soup)
汤

dàn huā tāng	egg-flower soup
báicài tāng	cabbage soup
xīhóngshì dàn tāng	tomato and egg soup
dōngguā tāng	white gourd soup
niúròu tāng	beef soup
xièròu tāng	crab soup
jī tāng	chicken soup
bèiké tāng	scallop soup
zhàcài tāng	pickled vegetable soup

Tiáowèiliào (seasoning)

yán	salt
hújiāo	pepper
yóu	oil
cù	vinegar
jièmo	mustard
jiàng yóu	soy sauce
táng	sugar
xiāng yóu	sesame oil
suàn	garlic
làjiāo yóu	pepper oil
làjiāo fěn	chili pepper

Zhūròu (pork)

tángcù páigǔ	sweet-and-sour spareribs
tángcù lǐjī	sweet-and-sour pork
shīzi tóu	pork meatballs
qīngjiāo ròusī	pork with green pepper
yúxiāng ròusī	spicy shredded pork
gānzhá zhūpái	fried pork fillet
chǎo zhūgān	stir-fried pork liver
chǎo yāohuār	stir-fried kidney

Niúròu (beef)

tángcù niúròu wán	sweet-and-sour meatballs
chǎo niúròu sī	stir-fried beef
gānbiān niúròu sī	dry-stir-fried beef
niúròu yángcōng	fried beef with onions
lóngxū niúròu	sliced beef with asparagus
hóngshāo niúròu	beef stew in soy sauce
gālí niúròu	curried beef
Měnggǔ kǎo ròu	Mongolian barbecue
háoyóu niúròu	beef with oyster sauce
qīngjiāo niúròu	shredded beef with peppers

FOLD HERE

Jīyā (poultry)

jī	chicken
yā	duck
chún	quail
yějī	pheasant
huǒjī	turkey
é	goose
gēzi	pigeon
chǎo jī sī	fried chicken shreds
gālí jī	curried chicken
yàoguǒ jīdīng	diced chicken with cashews
jī sī chǎo sǔn	fried chicken with bamboo shoots
zhāngchá yā	fried duck in spices
kǎo yā	roasted duck
cuìpí yā	crispy duck

Yǐnliào (beverages)

chá	tea
kāfēi	coffee
niúnǎi	milk
jiǔ	wine
píjiǔ	beer
shuǐ	water
kuàngquán shuǐ	mineral water
júzishuǐ	orange juice

FOLD HERE

Hǎixiān (seafood)

tǎyú	sole
guìyú	salmon
jìyú	perch
xuěyú	cod
lǐyú	carp
píngyú	turbot
pángxiè	crab
háo	oysters
xiān gānbèi	scallops
xiā	shrimp
lóngxiā	lobster
dàxiā	prawns
zhá dàxiā	fried shrimp
pēng dàxiā	braised prawns
zhá yú tiáo	fried fish slices
tángcù yú	sweet-and-sour fish
hóngshāo yú	sautéed fish in soy sauce
qīngzhēng yú	steamed Mandarin fish
tángcù huángyú	sweet-and-sour yellow fish
qīngzhēng xiè	steamed crab
xièfěn càixīn	crab with vegetables
miàntuō xiè	fried crab in batter
fúróng xiè	crab with egg
gōngbào xiārén	shrimp with hot peppers
xiè ròu dòufǔ	crabmeat with soy sauce

Dòu Fǔ (bean curd)

hóngshāo dòufǔ	bean curd with soy sauce
mápó dòufǔ	bean curd with pepper
dōnggū dòufǔ	bean curd with mushrooms
xiārén dòufǔ	bean curd with shrimp
mápó dòufǔ	bean curd with minced pork in hot sauce
shāguō dòufǔ	bean curd in casserole

(woh) **wǒ**	*(woh-muhn)* **wǒmen**
(nee) **nǐ**	*(nee-muhn)* **nǐmen**
(tah) **tā**	*(tah-muhn)* **tāmen**
(lie) **lái** *(woh)* *(lie)* **wǒ lái**	*(ssee-yoo-eh-ssee)* **xuéxí** *(woh)* *(ssee-yoo-eh-ssee)* **wǒ xuéxí**
(chee-oo) **qù** *(woh)* *(chee-oo)* **wǒ qù**	*(yoh)* **yǒu** *(woh)* *(yoh)* **wǒ yǒu**
(ssee-ahng) *(yow)* **xiǎng yào** *(woh)* *(ssee-ahng)* *(yow)* **wǒ xiǎng yào**	*(ssee-oo-yow)* **xūyào** *(woh)* *(ssee-oo-yow)* **wǒ xūyào**

we	I
you (plural)	you (singular)
they	he, she, it
to learn	to come
I learn	I come
to have	to go (to)
I have	I go
to need	would like
I need	I would like

(jee-ow)
jiào

(woh) *(jee-ow)*
wǒ jiào

(my)
mǎi

(woh) *(my)*
wǒ mǎi

(shwoh)
shuō

(woh) *(shwoh)*
wǒ shuō

(joo)
zhù

(woh) *(joo)*
wǒ zhù

(jee-ow)
jiào

(woh) *(jee-ow)*
wǒ jiào

(teeng-lee-oo)
tíngliú

(woh) *(teeng-lee-oo)*
wǒ tíngliú

(chr)
chī

(woh) *(chr)*
wǒ chī

(huh)
hē

(woh) *(huh)*
wǒ hē

(shwoh)
shuō

(woh) *(shwoh)*
wǒ shuō

(my)
mài

(woh) *(my)*
wǒ mài

(dwong)
dǒng

(woh) *(dwong)*
wǒ dǒng

(zi) *(shwoh)* *(yee-bee-ahn)*
zài shuō yíbiàn

(woh) *(zi)* *(shwoh)* *(yee-bee-ahn)*
wǒ zài shuō yíbiàn

to buy	to be called/named
I buy	I am called/named
to live/reside	to speak
I live/reside	I speak
to stay	to order
I stay	I order
to drink	to eat
I drink	I eat
to sell	to say
I sell	I say
to repeat	to understand
I repeat	I understand

(jow)
zhǎo

(woh) *(jow)*
wǒ zhǎo

(kahn-jee-ahn)
kànjiàn

(woh) *(kahn-jee-ahn)*
wǒ kànjiàn

(jee)
jì

(woh) *(jee)*
wǒ jì

(shway)
shuì

(woh) *(shway)*
wǒ shuì

(dah)
dǎ

(woh) *(dah)*
wǒ dǎ

(foo) *(chee-ahn)*
fù qián

(woh) *(foo)* *(chee-ahn)*
wǒ fù qián

(gay)
gěi

(woh) *(gay)*
wǒ gěi

(ssee-eh)
xiě

(woh) *(ssee-eh)*
wǒ xiě

(kahn)
kàn

(woh) *(kahn)*
wǒ kàn

(nung)
néng

(woh) *(nung)*
wǒ néng

(yeeng-gi)
yīnggāi

(woh) *(yeeng-gi)*
wǒ yīnggāi

(jihr-dow)
zhīdào

(woh) *(jihr-dow)*
wǒ zhīdào

to see	to look for
I see	I look for
to sleep	to send by mail
I sleep	I send by mail
to pay	to make
I pay	I make
to write	to give
I write	I give
to be able to/can	to read (books)
I can	I read
to know (fact)	to have to/should
I know	I have to/should

(ki)
kāi

(woh) *(ki)*
wǒ kāi

(fay)
fēi

(woh) *(fay)*
wǒ fēi

(loo-we-sseeng)
lǔxíng

(woh) *(loo-we-sseeng)*
wǒ lǔxíng

(zwoh)
zuò

(woh) *(zwoh)*
wǒ zuò

(hwahn) *(chuh)*
huàn chē

(woh) *(hwahn)* *(chuh)*
wǒ huàn chē

(dow)
dào

(woh) *(dow)*
wǒ dào

(shwoh-shr)
shōushi

(woh) *(shwoh-shr)*
wǒ shōushi

(ssee)
xǐ

(woh) *(ssee)*
wǒ xǐ

(deeng)
dìng

(woh) *(deeng)*
wǒ dìng

(shr)
shì

(woh) *(shr)*
wǒ shì

(gay) *(woh)*
gěi wǒ . . .

(dee-oo)
diū

(woh) *(dee-oo)*
wǒ diū

to fly

I fly

to sit/ride in

I sit/ride in

to arrive

I arrive

to wash

I wash

to be

I am

to lose

I lose

to leave/depart

I leave/depart

to travel

I travel

to transfer (vehicles)

I transfer

to pack

I pack

to book/reserve

I book/reserve

give me . . .

(jeen-tee-ahn)
jīntiān

(nee) *(how)* *(mah)*
Nǐ hǎo ma?

(zwoh-tee-ahn)
zuótiān

(cheeng)
qǐng

(meeng-tee-ahn)
míngtiān

(ssee-eh-ssee-eh)
xièxie

(zi-jee-ahn)
zàijiàn

(dway-boo-chee)
duìbùqǐ

(lao) *(sseen)*
lǎo – xīn

(dwoh-shao) *(chee-ahn)*
Duōshao qián?

(dah) *(ssee-ow)*
dà – xiǎo

(ki) *(gwahn-muhn)*
kāi – guānmén

How are you?	today
please	yesterday
thank you	tomorrow
excuse me/I'm sorry	good-bye
How much does this cost?	old - new
open - closed	big - small

(jee-ahn-kahng)   *(beeng)*

jiànkāng – bìng

(how)   *(hwhy)*   *(boo)*   *(how)*

hǎo – huài/bù hǎo

(ruh)   *(lung)*

rè – lěng

(dwahn)   *(chahng)*

duǎn – cháng

(gao)   *(dee)*

gāo – dī

(shahng)   *(ssee-ah)*

shàng – xià

(zwoh)   *(yoh)*

zuǒ – yòu

(mahn)   *(kwhy)*

màn – kuài

(lao)   *(nee-ahn-cheeng)*

lǎo – niánqīng

(gway)   *(pee-ahn-yee)*

guì – piányí

(chee-wong)   *(yoh-chee-ahn)*

qióng – yǒuqián

(dwoh)   *(shao)*

duō – shǎo

good - bad	healthy - sick
short - long	hot - cold
up - down	high - low
slow - fast	left - right
expensive-inexpensive	old - young
a lot - a little	poor - rich

Now that you've finished...

Congratulations

You've done it!

You've completed all the Steps, stuck your labels, flashed your cards and cut out your menu guide. Do you realize how far you've come and how much you've learned? You've accomplished what it could take years to achieve in a traditional language class.

You can now confidently

- ask questions,
- understand directions,
- make reservations,
- order food and
- shop anywhere.

And you can do it all in a foreign language! You can now go anywhere — from a large cosmopolitan restaurant to a small, out-of-the-way village where no one speaks English. Your experiences will be much more enjoyable and worry-free now that you speak the language and know something of the culture.

Yes, learning a foreign language can be fun. And no, not everyone abroad speaks English.

Kris Kershul

Kristine Kershul

* What about shipping costs?

STANDARD DELIVERY per address

If your items total	please add
up to $ 20.00	$5.00
$20.01 - $ 40.00	$6.00
$40.01 - $ 60.00	$7.00
$60.01 - $ 80.00	$8.00
$80.01 - $100.00	$9.00

If over $100, please call for charges.

For shipping outside the U.S., please call, fax or e-mail us at info@bbks.com for the best-possible shipping rates.

Dìngdān
order form

10 minutes a day® Series	QTY.	PRICE	TOTAL
ARABIC *in 10 minutes a day®*		$19.95	
CHINESE *in 10 minutes a day®*		$19.95	
FRENCH *in 10 minutes a day®*		$19.95	
GERMAN *in 10 minutes a day®*		$19.95	
HEBREW *in 10 minutes a day®*		$19.95	
INGLÉS *en 10 minutos al día®*		$19.95	
ITALIAN *in 10 minutes a day®*		$19.95	
JAPANESE *in 10 minutes a day®*		$17.95	
NORWEGIAN *in 10 minutes a day®*		$19.95	
PORTUGUESE *in 10 minutes a day®*		$18.95	
RUSSIAN *in 10 minutes a day®*		$19.95	
SPANISH *in 10 minutes a day®*		$18.95	
10 minutes a day AUDIO	**QTY.**	**PRICE**	**TOTAL**
SPANISH *in 10 minutes a day®* AUDIO		$59.95	
SPANISH AUDIO CDs only *(no book)*		$42.95	
Language Map Series	**QTY.**	**PRICE**	**TOTAL**
ARABIC *a language map®*		$7.95	
CHINESE *a language map®*		$7.95	
FRENCH *a language map®*		$7.95	
GERMAN *a language map®*		$7.95	
GREEK *a language map®*		$7.95	
HAWAIIAN *a language map®*		$7.95	
HEBREW *a language map®*		$7.95	
INGLÉS *un mapa del lenguaje®*		$7.95	
ITALIAN *a language map®*		$7.95	
JAPANESE *a language map®*		$7.95	
NORWEGIAN *a language map®*		$7.95	
POLISH *a language map®*		$7.95	
PORTUGUESE *a language map®*		$7.95	
RUSSIAN *a language map®*		$7.95	
SPANISH *a language map®*		$7.95	
VIETNAMESE *a language map®*		$7.95	

Item Total	
* Shipping	+
Total	
† Sales Tax	+
ORDER TOTAL	

† For delivery to individuals in Washington State, you must add 8.8% sales tax on the item total and the shipping costs combined. If your order is being delivered outside Washington State, you do not need to add sales tax.

Name _____

Address _____

_____

City _____ State _____ Zip _____

Day Phone (_____)_____

❏ My check or money order for $_____ is enclosed.

Please make checks and money orders payable to Bilingual Books, Inc.

❏ Bill my credit card ❏ VISA ❏ MC ❏ AMEX

No. _____ Exp. date ____/____

Signature _____

Send us this order form with your check, money order or credit card details. If paying by credit card, you may fax your order to **(206) 284-3660** or call us toll-free at **(800) 488-5068**. All prices are in US dollars and are subject to change without notice.

Bilingual Books, Inc. • **1719 West Nickerson Street Seattle, WA 98119 USA**

10 minutes a day® AUDIO

by Kristine K. Kershul

The *10 minutes a day*® AUDIO is based on the immensely successful *10 minutes a day*® Series. Millions of people around the world have used the *10 minutes a day*® Series for over two decades.

- Eight hours of personal instruction on six CDs.

- Use the CDs in combination with the companion book, and maximize your progress as you see AND hear the language.

- Listen to native speakers and practice right along with them.

- Suitable for the classroom, the homeschooler, as well as business and leisure travelers.

- The CDs in the *10 minutes a day*® AUDIO may also be purchased separately from the *10 minutes a day*® books.

Language Map® Series

by Kristine K. Kershul

These handy *Language Maps*® provide the essential words and phrases to cover the basics for any trip.

- Over 1,000 essential words and phrases divided into convenient categories.

- Laminated , folding design allows for quicker reference while resisting spills, tearing, and damage from frequent use.

- Durable, to hold up to being sat on, dropped, and stuffed into backpacks, pockets, and purses.

- An absolute must for anyone traveling abroad or studying at home.

For a list of available languages and ordering information, please see the order form on the previous page.